D1237771

THE WORLD OF
JACK AUBREY

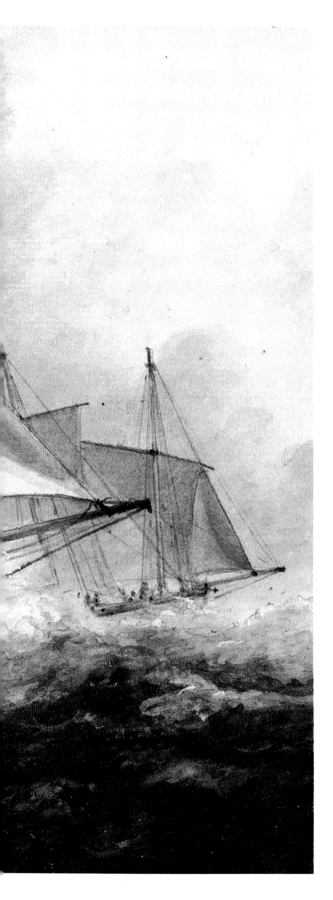

THE WORLD OF
JACK AUBREY

Twelve-pounders, Frigates, Cutlasses, and Insignia of
His Majesty's Royal Navy

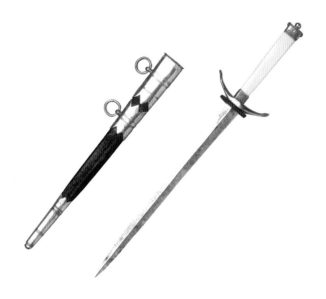

BY DAVID MILLER

AN IMPRINT OF RUNNING PRESS
PHILADELPHIA · LONDON

© 2003 Salamander Books Ltd
The Chrysalis Building
Bramley Road
London W10 6SP

A member of **Chrysalis** Books plc

This edition published in the United States by Courage Books, an imprint of
Running Press Book Publishers
125 South Twenty-second Street
Philadelphia, Pennsylvania 19103-4399

All rights reserved under the Pan-American and International Copyright Conventions.
Printed in China

This book may not be reproduced in whole or in part, in any form or by any means, electronic
or mechanical, including photocopying, recording, or by any information storage and retrieval
system or hereafter invented, without written permission from the publisher.

9 8 7 6 5 4 3 2 1

ISBN 0-7624-1652-1

CREDITS

Commissioning Editor: Stella Caldwell
Editor: Katherine Edelston
Designer: Q2A Solutions
Indexer: Alan Rutter
Production: Don Campaniello
Color Production: Anorax Imaging Ltd

This book may be ordered by mail from the publisher.
But try your bookstore first!

Visit us on the web!
www.runningpress.com

ADDITIONAL CAPTIONS

Page 1: Man in the main chains, heaving lead.
Page 2-3: A schooner close-hauled in a strong breeze.
Page 3: Midshipman's Dirk.
Page 4: Royal Navy Officer's Sea Service sword.
Page 5: Mr. Sharp, chief of the Brig, *Admiral Trowbrigde*;
barbarously wounded but put in leg irons.

CONTENTS

INTRODUCTION

ABOVE: A naval press-gang at work. Politicians and voters wanted a strong navy, but would not allow conscription, leaving the Admiralty with little alternative to the hated "press."

In the Jack Aubrey/Stephen Maturin novels Patrick O'Brian has created a unique pair of characters who develop as the series progresses. Naturally they use the language of the 18th century, which is, in itself, rich in its own idioms, but of greater importance is that much of their discussions are about maritime matters and thus full of some-

times confusing nautical technicalities.

This book is not a detailed reference book nor is it a concordance to the Jack Aubrey novels; those have already been written by Anthony Gary Brown, Dean King and others. Instead this book sets out to describe the naval environment in which the novels are set and to provide a companion which the reader can consult for information on ships, sailing and nautical matters. However, a complete handbook on the eighteenth century Royal Navy, its complex organisation, its vast array of ships, and how ships were rigged and sailed would take up many volumes, so this book concentrates on those elements that affected Captain Jack Aubrey.

It is not intended to overwhelm readers with a mass of statistical data, so where numbers of ships in service are given I have taken January 1805 as being reasonably typical; it was virtually the mid-point of the wars which lasted from 1793 to 1815 and was shortly before the Franco-Spanish defeat at Trafalgar, after which the strategic dominance of the Royal Navy was never in doubt. I have also taken particular care to identify and describe the real ships upon which Jack Aubrey's ships are based, so that the reader can see how closely fact and fiction are intertwined or, as in some cases, differ from the reality.

I hope that this book will add to the pleasure of Patrick O'Brian's many readers.

BELOW: This watercolor by a ship's chaplain shows the reality of a long cold night watch, with strong wind and heavy rain. The Master (with speaking trumpet), helmsman and lookouts wear long oilskins, the midshipman (foreground) has little protection, and the cabin-boy (right) has none at all.

CHAPTER I

RATED SHIPS

The Royal Navy classified its major warships according to a "rating" system, based on the number of long cannon carried. Thus a ship with 100 or more such cannon was a 1st rate, one with between 90 and 98 was a 2nd rate, and so on down to 20 guns which qualified as a 6th rate. Within these rates there was a major dividing line in that 3rd rates and above were "ships of the line" while 5th and 6th rates were frigates. All of these were three-masted vessels and the major difference lay in the number of gundecks, with 1st and 2nd rates having three, 3rd and 4th two and the remainder one (see table on page 11.)

The three-deckers, either 1st-rates with 100, 112, or 120 guns, and 2nd rates with 98, were the capital ships of their day; all were fitted as flagships and carried an admiral and his staff. But they were expensive and time-consuming to build, and once operational required enormous crews; as a

BELOW: HMS Hibernia (110), a three-decker First Rate. For some years the largest ship in the Royal Navy, Hibernia was 24ft longer and carried 10 more guns than Victory. Despite the pressure of war it took 14 years to build her, being commissioned in early 1805. She was almost invariably employed as a flagship and had a crew of almost a 1,000 men.

result they were always few in number.

The 3rd rates carried either 80, 74 or 64 guns, of which the 74s were by far the most numerous and successful, being designed to mount as many cannon for their size as possible and to be capable of taking on any ves-

sel in any navy and win. The 80s and 64s were much less satisfactory and reduced steadily in number as the war progressed. The 4th rate 50-60 guns and 5th rate 44-gun ships, all two-deckers, were particularly lacking, being insufficiently powerful to

BELOW: HMS Victory *(100 guns) was built at Chatham Dockyard and launched in 1765. She is still in full commission in Portsmouth, in 2003.*

ABOVE: The stern of a ship-of-the-line. The lanterns are at poop level and below is the gallery marking the after end of the captain's cabin, and below that is the wardroom. The surrounds are intricately carved as part of the ship's construction, although a wealthy captain may have added embellishments of his own.

Rate	Guns*	Type Name	Gun Decks	Crew**	In Service***		
					1794	1804	1814
First	100-120	Line	3	841	5 (1)	6 (1)	7 (0)
Second	90-98			743	9 (7)	11 (3)	5 (3)
Third	64-84		2	500-720	71 (24)	66 (29)	87 (16)
Fourth	50-60			350-420	8 (4)	12 (1)	8 (2)
Fifth	44			300-320	12 (3)	1 (1)	2 (0)
Fifth	28-44	Frigates	1	215-294	66 (3)	94 (18)	121 (11)
Sixth	20-28	Post-ship		121-195	32 (4)	19 (5)	22 (4)

The table header reads: **ROYAL NAVY RATING SYSTEM FOR MAJOR WARSHIPS**

* The Royal Navy counted carriage guns only and did not include swivel guns or carronades in this figure.

** Excluding admiral and his staff where employed as a flagship, and excluding "widow's men" in all cases (see Glossary).

*** The figures in brackets are those for ship "in ordinary"; i.e., in first-line reserve or undergoing refits. These figures do NOT include ships in "harbour service"; i.e., being employed as prison hulks, stores ships, etc.

RIGHT: HMS Victory (100) putting to sea. All the gunports are open and cannon run out for firing. The lowest gundeck is close to the waterline, limiting use of the leeward battery if the ship was heeling over.

ABOVE: Ships-of-the-line in the Downs, the center ship setting out on yet another voyage, probably to join a blockading squadron. Such ships were the backbone of the navy, the essence of British power.

RIGHT: HMS Hastings (74) lying "in ordinary" (i.e., in reserve). Topmasts, bowsprit and yards have been removed and the upper deck covered by an extensive awning, and only a small crew retained.

deserve a place in the line, although *Leander* (50) was in the line at Nelson's famous victory at the Battle of the Nile. In addition to this lack of firepower, these ships were not fast enough to serve as large frigates and as a type their numbers dropped steadily throughout the war years. The single-decked frigates, armed with between 28 and 44 guns, were fast, maneuverable and well-armed, being employed on independent operations, in a frigate squadron or as part of a major fleet. In the latter case they provided the commander-in-chief's reconnaissance force, their main mission being to find the enemy fleet, inform their admiral of its whereabouts and then

BELOW: HMS Cambrian, *a 40-gun frigate. The ropework of the standing and running rigging is apparent, but the ratlines and the gammoning on the bowsprit has been omitted for clarity.*

shadow it until it was brought to battle. There was an unwritten convention, obeyed scrupulously by all participants throughout the wars, that frigates were not to be touched in fleet encounters unless they themselves took the initiative. Thus the British frigate *Euryalus* was in the thick of the Battle of Trafalgar, but neither fired nor received a shot. On the other hand, while at the Battle of the Nile, the French frigate *Serieuse* fired at a British ship of the line, thus instantly losing its immunity and was blown out of the water.

Finally, there was the 6th rate post-ship, armed with either 20 or 24-guns, only marginally better armed than a sloop, but definitely too small to be recognised as a frigate. Below this came "unrated" vessels, ranging from 18-gun sloops , through brigs and schooners to gunboats, which are described in Chapter Two.

Like any system seeking to place objects in graduated categories, the Royal Navy's "rating system" was logical in general, but even the broadest of categorization into "ships of the line" and "frigates" was not totally precise, and the 4th and 5th rate two-deckers were sandwiched somewhat uncomfortably between them. Similarly, at the bottom end, the only real difference between a 6th rate and a sloop was that the Admiralty had decreed that one should be commanded by a post-Captain, the other by a Commander. The anomalies were even more apparent in the case of two very unusual vessels, *Arrow* and *Dart*, which were larger than 6th rates and carried 28 guns, but were classified as sloops; nevertheless, because of their unusual design and large size I have included them in this section.

There are three important points to be borne in mind when considering the number of guns suffixed to a ship's name which, at first sight, appears straightforward: e.g.,

RIGHT: A two-decker (left) and a frigate (right) make their way up the Thames estuary. Two-deckers were either Third (64-84 guns), Fourth (50-60) or Fifth (28-44) Rates, but only the 74-gun Thirrd Rates were considered of any real operational value.

RIGHT: Third-rate two-decker, HMS Worcester (64), was launched in 1769. She and her sisters were unpopular in service, and Worcester was reduced to a stores hulk at Deptford in 1788 and broken up there in 1816. The "64s" were considered to be seriously under-armed for their size and as a result had relatively short operational lives.

Worcester (64), *Boadicea* (38), etc. Firstly this gave no indication of the actual size of the guns, so for example, a "74's" main armament was 32-pounders, while a "64's" was 24-pounders—a considerable difference in capability. Secondly, all ships had a mix of weapons so that while a "64" mounted 64 guns, these were actually a mix of 24-pounders (26), 18-pounders (26) and 12-pounders (12). Thirdly, Royal Navy took cognisance only of long cannon and excluded carronades; thus, a British 5th rate completed in 1794 was described as a 38-gun vessel because she carried 28 18-pounders on the gun-deck and 10 9-pounders (six on the quarterdeck and four on the forecastle), but she also carried eight 32-pounder carronades, which simply did not count. Having explained the context, we now turn to the rated ships on which Jack Aubrey served in the course of the novels.

HMS *BELLONA*, 74

Nameship of her class, *Bellona*'s design by Sir Thomas Slade remained the basis of all British 74s for the next 20 years. Indeed, the 74 merited the title of "the backbone of the fleet," and its design was a happy compromise, being much cheaper than a three-decker, but with a very effective armament and good sailing qualities.

At the outbreak of the wars in 1792 *Bellona* was stationed in the Caribbean, but returned to England for a major refit at Plymouth in 1799. She served with the Channel Fleet in 1800-01, and in March 1801 was one of the fleet that sailed under Admiral Sir Hyde Parker to attack the main Danish naval base in Copenhagen. She was part of Nelson's squadron in the attack on 2 April, but was one of several ships that ran aground; she was able to use her guns

HMS *BELLONA*, 74
Rating: 3rd Rate.
Guns: 74.
Designer: Sir Thomas Slade.
Construction: Built at Chatham, Kent. Commissioned 1760.
Gundecks: 2.
Armament. Lower deck 28 x 32-pounder; upper deck 28 x 18-pounder; quarterdeck 14 x 9-pounder; forecastle 4 x 9-pounder.
Dimensions: Length 168 ft 0in; beam 46ft 11in; draught 19ft 9in.
Burthen: 1,615 tons.

LEFT: HMS Revenge *(74), a 2-decker Third Rate, taking the opportunity to dry her sails and to air the men's hammocks. Chatham—built and commissioned in 1805, she spent the next ten years in European waters imposing the British blockade which helped to tighten the noose around Napoleonic Europe.*

HMS *WORCESTER*, 64

Rating: 3rd Rate.

Guns: 64.

Gundecks: 2.

Construction: Portsmouth Dockyard. Completed 1769.

Armament: Lower deck – 26 x 24-pounder; upper deck – 26 x 18-pounder; quarterdeck – 10 x 9-pounder; forecastle - 2 x 9-pounder.

Dimensions: Length of gundeck 159ft 1 in; beam 44ft 6in; draught 18ft 11in.

Complement: 494.

Burthen: 1,380 tons.

ABOVE RIGHT: British frigate off Gibraltar in a stiff breeze (note the masthead pennant). The ship is taking in sail, difficult in such conditions, and requiring teamwork, training and coordination.

to a limited extent, although they were old and some burst, causing casualties.

Following a refit, *Bellona* returned to duty with the Channel Fleet, which included a foray to the Caribbean. She arrived back in Portsmouth in June 1802 at the time of the "short peace" when, like many ships, she was placed "in ordinary." When the war re-started in 1803 she was again refitted, returning to the fleet in late 1805. After a short spell with the Channel Fleet she went to North America where she was one of three ships to chance upon the storm-damaged and jury-rigged French *Imeptueaux* (74) making for a US port. They forced her to run aground and, the crew having been taken off, she was burnt.

Bellona operated in American waters until 1809 when she returned to the Channel Fleet. During the course of 1811-12 she was in the North Sea and in 1812/13 made a one-off voyage to St Helena, rejoining the Cherbourg blockade in May 1813. She was decommissioned in 1814 at Plymouth and broken up after 44 years service.

HMS *WORCESTER*, 64

The "64s" appeared in the middle of the 18th century and could be regarded as either cheaper-to-build and run versions of the 74-gun ship, or as more powerful "60s." They were designated "line-of-battle-ships" but the simple classification as a "64" disguised the fact that they were armed with 24-pounders on the lower deck compared with 32-pounders in the larger ships which made them inferior in weight of broadside by a considerable margin—600lb compared to 880lb. They were, however, of value in the more distant waters of the growing empire.

They were always regarded as lacking in firepower and had a relatively short operational life. Most were put "in ordinary" or converted to stores ships following the end of the American War of Independence and on the outbreak of war in 1793 there were just two in service, 28 "in ordinary" and 13 employed as stores ships, harbor ships and other non-operational tasks. A few were then brought back into service, but they were still unpopular and were generally employed in secondary duties, being kept out of the major fleets wherever possible, although *Ardent* and *Polyphemus* were both present at the Battle of Copenhagen in 1801.

Worcester was typical, being commissioned in 1769 and participating in the Battle of Ushant in 1778. She served in the Indian Ocean in 1779-83 but was one of those converted to stores hulks in 1788 and was broken up there in December 1816.

HMS *LEOPARD*, 50

A fair number of 4th rate, two-deck ships were built in the first half of the 18th century, but the 50-gun ships were officially taken out of "the line" in the middle of the century, leaving them with a somewhat indeterminate status. Despite this some new construction was started in the 1770s, mainly for employment as flagships for small squadrons, particularly in distant waters in peacetime, but after a number had been laid down the work was suspended. *Leopard* was one of these, being laid down at Portsmouth Dockyard in 1775, but when work stopped her frames lay there for almost a decade until they were removed to Sheerness, where work was restarted and she was relaunched in 1790, 15 years after being laid down!

Leopard was at the Nore in 1797 when the mutiny took place. Her captain and some of the officers were sent ashore, but when it was proposed by the mutineers' committee aboard another ship that the fleet should be handed over to the French, *Leopard*'s crew was the first to return to duty. In July 1799 *Leopard* sailed for India wearing the flag of Rear-Admiral John Blankett, escorting a convoy of East Indiamen. She remained there for several years, one highlight being the capture of a French privateer, operating out of Mauritius.

Leopard returned to England in February 1803 to enter Chatham dockyard for a refit which was completed in 1804, and she then spent many months as a flagship in the Channel. In 1806 she sailed for North America and Halifax station, and the following summer found her lying in the Chesapeake River with several other British ships blockading two French 74s and waiting for them to come out. A large group of seamen (some of them United States citizens, others British) seized the opportunity to flee ashore and desert and it soon became known to the British authorities that many of these had been recruited into the large frigate, USS *Chesapeake* (36) which led the British admiral to issue an order that if the

---

HMS *LEOPARD*, 50
Rating: 4th Rate.
Guns: 50.
Gundecks: 2.
Construction.
Completed Sheerness Dockyard, 1790.
Designer: Sir John Williams.
Armament: Lower deck - 22 x 24-pounder; upper deck - 22 x 12-pounder; quarterdeck - 4 x 6-pounder; forecastle - 2 x 6-pounder.
Dimensions: Length 146ft beam 30.5ft; draught 17.5ft
Burthen: 1,045 tons.
Complement: 350.

US frigate was sighted outside American territorial waters it was to be stopped and searched, and any deserters arrested. *Leopard* sighted the *Chesapeake* on 22 June, some 12 miles off Cape Henry and sent a messenger requesting permission to carry out a search. US Commodore Barron refused, whereupon Captain Humphreys put a shot across the American ship's bow and when this failed to have the desired effect fired three rounds into her, killing three men, wounding 18 and causing considerable damage. *Chesapeake* was unprepared and after firing a token single round, complied, and the British duly found four deserters, who were removed. The American government was understandably furious and President Jefferson ordered that all British armed vessels must leave US waters immediately.

Having achieved diplomatic notoriety, *Leopard* returned home and in 1808 sailed to the Indian Ocean again where she served for a time as flagship of Vice-Admiral Bertie, but returned to England in 1810, by now thoroughly worn out as a man-of-war. She was, therefore, taken in hand at Chatham dockyard and converted into a troopship, the space for the soldiers' accommodation and stores being created by a major reduction in her armament. She then operated for many months off the Iberian coast supporting Wellington's Peninsular army, but returned to England again in 1814. She next carried a battalion of the Scots Guards to Canada, but ran aground in the Gulf of St. Lawrence on 28 June 1814; none of the crew or passengers were lost, but the ship was completely destroyed.

HMS *DIANA*

Diana was completed at Rotherhithe in 1794 and was the last of a group of Royal Navy frigates built on the lines of the French *Hébé*, a 40-gun ship captured in 1782. She was built of oak, the main beams being well over 12 inches square, while the planking was about 5 inches thick. Impressive as this was a cannon ball would smash through the planking, generating a cloud of splinters and it was these that caused by far the greatest number of casualties.

Like all frigates *Diana* had a very busy war. After a period in home waters she went to the Caribbean in 1799 and then to the Mediterranean. In 1807 she was operating out of Ireland and on February 18 took a large French privateer some 100 miles south-west of the isles of Scilly after a five hour chase. In 1809 she was in the Brazils and brought home from Rio de Janeiro one of the navy's more colorful (and unpopular officers) Rear-Admiral Sir Sidney Smith. *Diana* was immediately assigned to the ill-fated Walcheren operation where, in an unusual maneuver, her boats captured a complete French army artillery battery, with its guns, men, and ammunition.

In 1810 *Diana* was once more on blockade duties in the Channel when she was one of four British frigates which attacked two French frigates trying to escape from Boulogne. One of the French vessels was forced to run itself ashore, but *Elize* anchored under the guns of a coastal battery. On the night of December 23/24 a small party in a boat took combustible materials, boarded *Elize* and, despite heavy fire from the fortress and nearby French ships set her on fire, not leaving until her total destruction was assured. In 1811 *Diana* was involved in an adventurous undertaking in the mouth of the Gironde, which involved two British ships entering the river flying the French flag and operating for some hours capturing various prizes before the deception was revealed.

LEFT: A British frigate. Such ships were the Royal Navy's maids-of-all-work, always busying themselves about tasks for which the line-of-battle ships were too large or too slow.

HMS _Diana_
Rating: 5th Rate.
Guns. 38.
Construction: Randall, Rotherhithe.
Armament: Upper deck – 28 x 18-pounder; quarterdeck – 6 x 9-pounder, 6 x 32-pounder carronade; forecastle – 4 x 9-pounder, 2 x 32-pounder carronade.
Dimensions: Length 146ft 0in; beam 39ft 0in; draught 15ft 0in.
Tonnage: 984 tons.
Complement: 280.

HMS _LIVELY_, 38
Rating: 5th Rate.
Guns: 38.
Gun decks: 1.
Designer: Sir William
Rule.
Construction:
Woolwich Dockyard.
Commissioned 1804.
Armament: Main
deck – 28 x 18-
pounder; quarterdeck
– 2 x 9-pounder, 12 x
32-pounder
carronades; forecastle
– 2 x 9-pounder long
guns, 2 x 32-pounder
carronades.
Dimensions: Length
154ft 0in; beam 39ft
5in; draught 13ft 6in.
Burthen: 1,073 tons.
Complement: 284.

In 1812 _Diana_, worn out by 14 years of constant operations, was placed "in ordinary." She underwent a thorough refit in 1813-14, but when the wars ended in 1815 she was sold to the Dutch government.

HMS _LIVELY_, 38

Lively was built at the Woolwich Dockyard and completed in 1804, and then spent her whole operational life either in the Mediterranean or in the Atlantic off the Iberian coast. Soon after joining the fleet she was involved in a famous incident when, as part of a squadron of four frigates, she took part in an attack on a Spanish squadron, also of four frigates. At that time England and Spain were technically at peace, although it was known that the French, with whom Britain was at war, were assisting the Spanish government in various ways, including financial.

It was known that the fabled Spanish treasure fleet was at sea and the British government issued orders for it to be intercepted and detained, but not to be attacked, unless it fired first. The British duly found the Spanish squadron, also composed of four frigates, and when the two were sailing abreast and some 30 yards apart the British fired a shot across the bows of the leading Spanish vessel. A boat was sent across to the Spanish flagship to tell the admiral that his ships were to be detained, but he refused to comply and, considering his ships to be threatened (a correct assessment!) his ships opened fire on the British.

One of the Spanish ships, the frigate _Mercedes_ (34) blew up killing all but some 40 of her crew who survived for a while on the bow section which remained afloat for a few minutes. Two other Spanish ships then surrendered but the flagship attempted to escape, only to be overtaken by _Lively_, which was well-known as a very fast sailer.

As in so many engagements, the English casualties were very small, with only two killed and seven wounded, but the Spanish lost 260 men (240 of them aboard _Mercedes_) and 80 wounded. The action was controversial because war had not been declared, so the British government decided that it was a "police action" enabling it to grab far more of the prize money than if it had taken place in war.

Lively continued her operations, which included rescuing all the crew and passengers from a sinking brig in November 1807 and giving direct support to British Army units ashore in 1809.

Lively was considered to be an excellent vessel, being both very fast and weatherly. In trials she demonstrated a maximum speed of 13 knots off wind and 11 knots close-hauled, but it was considered that she performed somewhat better in heavy weather, less well in light winds. She was thought slightly "stiff" but "dependable in stays" (i.e., she went about without difficulty).

Like so many contemporary English frigates, _Lively_ was wrecked, in her case on rocks on the shore of Malta on August 26 1810, but without any loss of life.

HMS _BOADICEA_, 38

The British 38-gun frigate design was basically a 36-gun design with an extra two guns on the upper deck. The first two such ships were the Minerva-class of four vessels, built in 1780-82, but these were found to be too small for the number of weapons, and the next group, Artois-class, although a little larger was no better. Then, in 1782, the British captured the French frigate, _Hébé_, which was a better design and was placed in production in English yards as the Leda-class, of which no less than 49 were built. British designers still sought to produce a successful British design, which led to *Naiad* and *Amazon*, which were satisfactory but by no means outstanding. Next the British captured the French 38-gun frigates *Pomone* and *Imperieuse* and copied these, but to British standards, with better scantlings and fastenings, and one of these was the *Boadicea*.

Boadicea, completed at Buckler's Hard in 1797, achieved her first success on August 14 that year when she captured the Spanish ship *Union* (22) en route from Corunna to Buenos Aires. She then moved to the Channel taking a number of prizes, including one curiosity, the French vessel *Bombard No 69*, a specialist vessel built some years earlier for the invasion of England. This curiosity was intended to carry one 13 inch mortar, one long 24-pounder and some swivel guns, together with 150 soldiers, all on a draught of a mere 42 inches. Unsurprisingly it required little effort for *Boadicea* to take it.

She continued to take prizes: *Neptuno* (20) and a merchantman cut out of Corunna, and at sea, a privateer and a despatch vessel, *Vautour* (12) which was carrying official mail. Routine duties continued, including escorting a convoy to Barbados in 1803, but in 1806 she took part in a more unusual and arduous duty, protecting English whalers in the Davis Straits, which she repeated the following year.

In 1808 *Boadicea* sailed for the Indian Ocean, remaining there for three years. In September 1809 she took part in an operation against Reunion island, an amphibious force being landed, which eliminated artillery batteries, enabling the ships to enter the bay, capture the French frigate *Caroline* (46) and retake two East India Company vessels. A second operation was mounted in July 1810 when *Boadicea* was part of a force carrying some 4,200 troops to attack Reunion again, and after some not very effective resistance the French surrendered on July 9.

In November 1810 Vice-Admiral Bertie led another amphibious operation, this time to take Mauritius and the landing force, commanded by Major-General Abercrombie, landed and then marched on Port Louis, supplied by the fleet as it advanced. The French capitulated on December 7, the prizes including six frigates, three brigs, five gunboats, and 28 merchantmen, while three East India Company vessels were recaptured. Captain Rowley and *Boadicea* had the honor of carrying Admiral Bertie's

HMS *BOADICEA*, 38
Rating: 5th
Guns: 38.
Construction: Adams, Buckler's Hard. Commissioned 1797.
Armament: Main deck—28 x 18pounder; quarterdeck—8 x 9-pounder, 6 x 32-pounder carronades; forecastle—2 x 9 pounder, 2 x 32-pounder carronades.
Dimensions: Length 148ft 6in; beam 39ft 8in; draught 12ft 8in.
Burthen: 1,038 tons.
Complement: 284.

Division	Boat	Commander	Crew	Mission
\ **BOAT CREWS FOR HMS *SURPRISE* ATTACK (SEE PAGE 24)**				
#1 Starboard	Pinnace	Captain	18	Starboard gangway
	Launch	Lieutenant	25	Bow. Cut cable. Set foretopsail
	Jolly boat	Midshipman	9	Quarterdeck. Cut cable. Set mizen topsail
#2 Larboard	Gig	Surgeon	16	Larboard bow
	Cutter	Lieutenant	17	Larboard gangway
	Cutter	Boatswain	16	Larboard quarter
TOTALS	6	6	101	

despatches back to England. *Boadicea* saw out the remainder of the war in home waters.

HMS *SURPRISE*, 28

Originally named *L'Unité*, she was one of a class of five 24-gun corvettes built for the French Navy. She was completed in 1794, but after less than two years service was captured in the Mediterranean by HMS *Inconstant* (April 20 1796) and taken into British service. Following her capture she was sent to England where she was renamed HMS *Surprise* (there was already a *L'Unité* in the Royal Navy) and was also rearmed, her 24 long guns being replaced by 24 x 32-pounder carronades on the gun-deck, and 8 x 32-pound carronades on the quarterdeck, but with just four long 6-pounders on her forecastle. Because carronades were not counted, there was some difficulty in placing her in the rating system; initially declared equivalent to a 28-gun ship and classified as a 5th rate, less than a year later she was reclassified as a 6th rate.

She left England for Jamaica in July 1796 under her new commanding officer, Captain Edward Hamilton. French-built frigates were very popular with British crews as their maneuverability and speed were better than those of their British-designed equivalents. Even so, Captain Hamilton had her re-rigged in the Bermuda navy yard, where she was outfitted with the mainmast and the associated yards and rigging for a British 36-gun frigate, giving her even greater speed than would otherwise have been the case. His reasoning may have been that while her carronades provided very powerful short-range firepower, most enemies would simply sit outside their range and pound away; thus the extra sail area would enable him to close on his targets at a much greater speed and enable him

to take advantage of his powerful short-range firepower.

Surprise had a series of successes in October 1799. There were two captures, the first of a French schooner, *Nancy*, carrying a cargo of coffee, the second of a 10-gunned Dutch privateer with the unfortunate name of *Lame Duck*, which was cut out from Aruba harbor. The third was the destruction of the *Manuel*, a Spanish schooner destroyed near Porto Cavallo.

Next came the famous exploit, in which she recovered the former HMS *Hermione* (32) whose whole crew had mutinied and handed her over to the Spanish. *Surprise* found her lying in Porto Cabalo, some 70 miles west of Caracas, Venezuela, where she presented a daunting prospect: *Hermione* was in a good repair, armed with 44 long guns and with a crew of some 392 men, and lying within range of some 200 shore guns. Having weighed up the risks, Hamilton attacked, dividing his attacking party into two divisions (see table on page 23).

Various difficulties arose, but the attack was an outstanding success. *Hermione* was recovered, and both ships headed for an

HMS *SURPRISE*, 28
Rating: 6th Rate.
Guns. 28 (nominal).
Construction:
Completed in Le Havre, France as L'Unité, corvette, 1794.
Armament: As completed, 24 x 9-pounder long guns. After capture was re-armed by Royal Navy with: gundeck - 24 x 32-pounder carronades; quarterdeck - 8 x 32-pounder carronades; forecastle - 4 x long 6-pounder.
Dimensions: Length of gundeck 126ft.
Burthen: 579 tons.
Complement: 198.

ecstatic welcome in Jamaica. The Spanish lost 119 killed and 97 wounded, while the British had no losses and only 12 wounded, one of the heroes of the affair being the ship's surgeon, John M'Mullen, who should not have been an active participant, but who nevertheless led an assault party and wielded his sword with the best. *Surprise* returned to England in late 1801.

Surprise's design was not too popular with the Royal Navy. One criticism was that she was "little more than a quarterdeck corvette" and another that she carried too heavy an armament for her size. It may have been a combination of such remarks that led to her being sold at Deptford in February 1802, when she was only eight years old, a comparatively short operational life for a contemporary warship, particularly a well built French one.

BELOW: The frigate HMS Nymph (36) was captured from the French in 1780. Here she passes the Round Tower on Portsmouth Point, outward bound to face unknown dangers and undreamt-of adventures.

CHAPTER II

UNRATED VESSELS

The term "unrated" covered a wide variety of smaller vessels, but while the stately ships-of-the-line fought the great fleet actions and the dashing frigates conducted many glorious actions, it was the hundreds of smaller vessels that kept the whole Royal Navy machine going. These vessels carried out the dozens of mundane tasks, many of them dreary and repetitive, such as inshore patrols and convoy escorts, but without which the naval war would have come to a halt. Only rarely did one of these vessels come to public attention, but when they did—such as

schooner *Pickle* bringing the despatch home from Trafalgar or the fireships at Basque Roads—the rewards were richly deserved.

Sloop-of-war

"Sloop-of-war" was term which covered four major variations, but the basic distinction were that they were slightly smaller than 6th rate frigates and were commanded by a commander rather than a post-captain. Within these limits there were "quarterdeck sloops" which had both a quarterdeck and a forecastle, and "flush-decked sloops"

RIGHT: The quarterdeck, ship-rigged sloop, HMS Blossom (16), launched in 1806; standing and running rigging are identical with that of a frigate, but on a smaller scale. Blossom operated in the Atlantic and Mediterranean during the war, but her most remarkable exploit came when, between May 1825 and September 1828, she sailed 73,000 miles on a single, continuous voyage, mainly in the Pacific and north to the Bering Straits. She is seen here visiting the Sandwich Islands, May 19-31, 1826.

ROYAL NAVY SLOOPS - JANUARY 1805						
Class	Variations	Guns	In commission	In ordinary	Building	Total
Ship-rigged (3 masts)	Quarterdeck	18	10	1	1	12
		16	17	1	7	25
		14	2	0	0	2
	Flush-decked	18	19	0	2	21
		16	14	0	0	14
		14	13	0	0	13
Brig-rigged (2 masts)	Flush-decked	18	27	0	9	36
		16	12	0	0	12
		14	3	0	0	3
Arrow/Dart*	Experimental	28	2	0	0	2
TOTALS			119	2	19	140

* These were to a special design; see pages 34-37.

which had neither, the upper deck being continuous from the stem to the stern. The other two variations were that some were "ship-rigged" (i.e., three masted), while the others were "brig-rigged" (i.e., two masted).

For all, their tasks included commerce protection, inshore defensive patrols around the coasts of the British Isles against invasion and smugglers, as well as offensive patrols along enemy shores. However, they were not suited to working with the fleet as a sort of cheaper frigate, for two reasons. First, their armament was weaker and, secondly, they were relatively slow, so they were not only incapable of defending themselves against enemy frigates, their most likely foe in such a role, but they were also unable to outrun them. The great majority of sloops were armed with carronades which gave good firepower—but only at short range.

Quarter-deck ship-rig sloops were both physically and visually slightly smaller version of 6th rate post-ships, and most of the early vessels had 18 guns on upper deck plus swivel guns on quarterdeck and forecastle. During the Napoleonic wars it became more common to mount carronades and the Conway-class of 18 vessels built from 1805 onwards were armed with 18 32-pounder carronades on the upper deck and six 12-pounder carronades on the quarterdeck, while the forecastle carried two 12-pounder carronades but with the addition of two 6-pounder long guns to serve as chasers. There were 39 such vessels in the Navy List in 1805 (see table above) and 57 at the end of the war in 1815.

The first of the flush-decked sloops was completed in 1796 and the numbers increased rapidly thereafter, with 43 in service in 1801 and 48 in 1805. They were more weatherly than the quarterdeck sloops, but the main loss was in the quality of officer accommodation, particularly for the captain. The type fell out of favor, and only 20 were left in service in 1815.

Brig-rigged sloops had two masts and the Cruizer- and Snake-class sloops were identical in virtually all respects except that the former had two masts and the latter three. In fact 104 Cruizer-class sloops were built, giving them the distinction of being the largest single group of sailing warships ever built for any navy. Some were built in oak, others in fir and a few in teak.

Gun-Brigs

BELOW: HM Brig, Ariel (18), completed in 1806, served in the Baltic and North Seas 1807-14. Brigs were small but very useful, carrying out a host of duties; the captain was normally a Lieutenant and Commander.

The gun-brig was a slightly smaller version of the brig-sloop, and commanded by a lieutenant rather than a commander. Most brigs were armed with 14 24-pounder carronades, although some of the later vessels had 14 18-pounder carronades with two long 6-pounders as chasers. Some gun-brigs were taken up directly from trade to meet a current shortage, particularly overseas,

such as HMS *Nancy* at Buenes Aires in 1811 which was bought to serve as a despatch vessel between the two main bases in Rio de Janeiro and Buenos Aires, but most were built to Admiralty designs. By definition, a brig had two masts, both square-rigged, but with a fore-and-aft, gaff-rigged driver on the main mast. A similar design, known as a snow, also had a gaff-headed main course, the difference between them—and a very fine one—being that the brig's main course was hoisted directly on the mainmast, while in the snow it was raised on a rope horse.

Bombs

When warships attacked forts they had to approach close enough for their long guns to be effective, but this not only brought them within range of the fortress's guns, it

also meant that they could not elevate their guns sufficiently to fire a plunging shot into the interior of the fortress. One solution was to use mortars, these were large and very heavy weapons with considerable recoil, which required a heavy mounting and a vessel rigged in such a way that the weapons could fire at high angle. This led to the specialized design—the "bomb." A number served with the fleet during the years 1793-1815, and 17 were in commission in 1805. Some were employed at Copenhagen and others during the Walcheren campaign in 1809, while at least one was used against the United States in the War of 1812 and, together with the Congreve rocket, was immortalized in the lines of the US National Anthem, "...and the rockets red glare and the bombs burst-

ing in the air." Bomb vessels were manned by Royal Navy crews, but the mortar itself was crewed by men of the Royal Artillery, who came not from the army but the military forces of the Board of Ordnance. Each bomb was normally accompanied by an auxiliary vessel carrying extra rounds and providing accommodation.

Fireships

Fireships were packed with combustibles and taken by a skeleton crew to a point where they could either sail or drift down into an enemy fleet at anchor, whereupon the crew would light the fuses and take to the boats. A small number of purpose-built fireships were in service during the war from 1792 to 1815. The operational prob-

ABOVE: A bomb ketch. Such vessels were armed with a heavy mortar, which was located in a well, forward of the mainmast. Note the minimal rigging forward, which was intended to give the weapon as great a field-of-fire as possible.

ideal target for fireships. When purpose-built fireships failed to arrive in time eight transports, including *Mediator* (44), an ex-Indiaman bought into the fleet in 1804, were packed with combustibles (mainly tar and resin), while another three were converted for use as explosive ships, with combustibles in the holds topped with explosive and all capped with sand and bricks to force the explosion out sideways rather than upwards. The force also included three small ships fitted out to fire Congreve rockets and Aetna, a bomb, all intended to add to the enemy's confusion. It was not until April 11 that all was ready but then, with a strong north-westerly blowing and a very favorable four knot tide, the attack force under the command of Captain Lord Cochrane started to sail down on their unsuspecting targets. Not all went as planned but sufficient ships broke through the defensive boom, ignited and got in among the French fleet, panicking their crews; within two hours 13 French ships had been run aground.

ABOVE: In the right circumstances fireships were extremely effective, but required nice judgement by the captain, who had to ensure that his ship would sail its own way into the enemy line before he set fire to the combustibles and took the boats with his crew. At the Battle of Basque Roads on the night of April 11, 1809, seen here, eight transports were converted into fireships and used against the French fleet, which had no option but to withdraw, with no less than 13 of them running aground.

lem, however, was that they required very particular conditions—a large target fleet at anchor and the correct combination of tide and wind—which were seldom met.

One famous opportunity did, however, arise in 1809 when a British squadron of three ships-of-the-line and a frigate found a French fleet of 14 ships-of-the-line at anchor in the Basque Roads, providing an

RIGHT: A schooner sailing close-hauled in a stiff breeze. It is completely fore-and-aft rigged and would have sailed much closer to the wind than a square-sailed vessel.

Schooners

A schooner normally had two masts, with gaff-rigged courses, square topsails on the foremast, and one or more jibs, but there were also a few with three masts, known as tern schooners. The design originated in the early 1700s and proved fine sailers, but were not adopted by the Royal Navy until 1796-7 when Samuel Bentham (the designer of *Arrow* and *Dart*) designed four schooners which, as usual with this man, were of revolutionary design, and (again as usual) were not received with any great enthusiasm.

Some other schooners were built in Bermuda and although they were fast and sailed well (with excellent performance to windward) they were weakly armed and were mainly employed as despatch vessels and advice boats. One schooner, HMS *Pickle*, attained undying fame when she carried home the news of Nelson's victory at Trafalgar. One of the most successful schooners of this period was the American *Prince de Neufchatel*, which was noted for her very high speed, which enabled her to escape superior Royal Naval forces on at least one occasion.

Gunboats

Gunboats were small craft, either sail- or oar-powered (sometimes both), armed with

ABOVE: An armed topsail schooner. Such vessels were fast sailers, but had only a light armament, and were generally used as despatch or advice boats, carrying messages and important passengers.

one or two heavy guns at either end, normally capable of firing only dead ahead or astern, since the vessel was unable to absorb the recoil in any other direction without capsizing. They were employed in harbors and inshore waters, but were of little use, although occasionally large numbers of them could overpower a brig or sloop, especially if the latter was becalmed and was situated not too far from the shore.

Ship's Boats

Small boats were essential for movement when in harbor, carrying people and stores between ships and the shore, or between one ship and another. They were also used

LEFT: All warships carried a number of various types of ship's boats to transport people and stores between ship and shore, or between ships. This is a senior officer's barge, with a carved transom and decorated gunwales.

TYPICAL BOATS CARRIED BY ROYAL NAVY SHIPS 1792-1815					
Rate	Barge	Launch	Pinnace	Cutter	Totals
1st	1	2	2	3	8
2nd	1	2	2	3	8
3rd	0	1	2	3	6
4th	0	1	1	3	5
5th	0	1	1	3	5
6th	0	1	1	1-2	3-4
Unrated	0	1	1	1	3

(Note: The numbers would have fluctuated, depending in part upon the captain's preferences and also on what was available)

to conduct security patrols around the ship in a foreign port, sometimes to prevent the enemy from approaching, but on other occasions to prevent the ship's own sailors from "running" (deserting). They also operated between ships when at sea, rescued men who had fallen overboard and, perhaps most important of all, were absolutely essential for amphibious landings and cutting-out parties, in the course of which they were sometimes rowed prodigious dis-

tances. Another role was to assist in the movement of a ship, for example, by towing in a calm or by moving the anchors (a process known as "kedging"). The boats were stowed aboard the parent ship, usually resting on the spare spars and well clear of those working on the deck, although in battle they were sometimes towed astern. There was, however, no question of them being regarded as ship's lifeboats in the modern sense.

RIGHT: The brig, HMS Penguin (16), bought by the Admiralty in 1795 and sold out of the service in 1809. An exceptionally handsome vessel, she gives the impression of speed and purposefulness, accentuated by the marked rake on the mainmast.

Admirals' and captains' barges were of particular importance, since the smartness of the boat, and the appearance and performance of the crew were frequently the standards by which their ships were judged. The captain of HMS *Niger*, for example, outfitted his boat's crew with completely black uniforms. These boats were also useful in providing midshipmen with their first experience of a semi-independent command, requiring both seamanship and control of a crew.

Royal Navy warships tended to carry more boats than those in foreign navies, possibly because they spent far longer at sea and went on much longer voyages. Most imposing was the barge and although in the civilian world a barge was a large, slow-moving cargo carrier, in the navy the word was used to describe a long, light rowing vessel specifically intended for senior officers, such as post-captains and admirals. It could be up to 36 feet in length and have a crew of 12 oarsmen plus the helmsman and bowman.

The pinnace was similar in design to the barge, but smaller and was usually reserved for more junior officers; there was at least one in 36-gun ships and larger. The launch had a greater beam, which not only made it more seaworthy but also gave it greater carrying capacity; they were, typically, some 30-32 feet in length, and could carry loads such as a dozen filled water-butts.

Cutters were good sailing boats and usually clinker built. The jolly-boat (also known as a skiff) was a smaller version of the cutter and was a multi-purpose workhorse. The gig was a light, narrow boat, sometimes used for commanders of smaller vessels. Smallest of all was the dinghy, a term that was imported from India.

Hired Vessels

Some types of vessel were hired for a specific purpose, and then most usually for a specified period of time. Hired vessels included transports, bomb tenders, and the like, which continued to be manned by their

ABOVE: The five larger vessels with masts are American sailing gunboats, each armed with a small number of cannon, and are being attacked by British ships' boats, each with a carronade in the bows. This action, on December 14, 1814 was possible because the American gunboats had run aground, and involved some 1,200 sailors and Royal Marines in 42 boats. Throughout the Napoleonic wars sailing ships, lying becalmed, aground or at anchor, were vulnerable to such attacks by small boats.

HM Sloop *Ariel*

Rating: sloop.

Guns: 18

Construction:
Completed 1806.

Armament: 18 x 4-
pounder.

Dimensions: Length
106ft beam 28ft.

Burthen: 367 tons.

Complement: 124

civilian crews. In other cases, however, civilian vessels were purchased for more warlike employment and several Honorable East India Company ships were purchased and converted into 64-gun ships-of-the-line.

HM SLOOP *ARIEL*

There was an earlier HMS *Ariel*, also a sloop armed with 16 guns, which was launched in 1782 and sold in August 1802. That vessel cannot, however, have been Aubrey's vessel, since in "The Surgeon's Mate" he returns to England after the fight between HMS *Shannon* and USS *Chesapeake*, which took place on June 1, 1813.

As sometimes happened, there was a second *Ariel* in the Navy List over the same period. This was a teak-built brig, completed in Bombay Dockyard in 1809. Armed with 14 guns and with a burthen of 160 tons, she served her entire career in Eastern waters, and foundered there in 1820. This clearly cannot have been Aubrey's vessel, either. Thus, the *Ariel* which Aubrey commanded must have been that launched in 1809, as described above. This vessel served in the North Sea from 1807 to 1810 when she went to the Baltic. After several years service there she was sent to North America in 1814 and returned to England in 1816, where she was sold.

HM SLOOPS *ARROW/DART*, 28 (HM SLOOP *POLYCHREST*)

It is often claimed that during the wars of 1793-1815 the Admiralty was conservative, doing little to encourage technological advance, but there were numerous experiments. One such was a design from two remarkable men: Brigadier-General Sir Samuel Bentham and Captain John Schank, RN, which resulted in two identical and highly unusual ship-rigged sloops, *Arrow* and *Dart*.

Bentham (1757-1831) had spent many years as a naval architect on the Continent and in Russia but returned to England in 1795 and immediately offered his services to the British Admiralty. He must have been most persuasive, since the appointment of Inspector-General of Naval Works was created especially for him and, despite the demands of wartime construction programs, the Admiralty also gave him permission to build seven vessels to test his ideas.

The other participant in these designs was Captain John Schank, RN, a prolific inventor. One of his inventions was the "sliding keel" which had been tested in the two-masted *Trial Cutter* sailing out of Teignmouth, Devon, in 1789-91, a notoriously difficult harbor entrance, but *Trial* was enthusiastically reported on by her crew.

Arrow and *Dart* embodied many innovations from both men, with Bentham responsible for the overall hull design, which was of a unique shape. Contemporary ships had a vertical stem and when viewed from above their bow had a blunt, rounded planform, the harshness of these lines being alleviated only by the very narrow, raked cutwater. Bentham's design had a raked bow, which in planform led to a sharp point; it was, in fact, almost identical to the shape employed in modern ships. Even more unusual was that the stern was of a similarly shape and was strictly functional with no stern walk or decoration, giving rise to the comment that the design was "double-ended." These two ships also had a very unusual "wedge-shaped" cross-section, increasing above the

MISCELLANEOUS SMALLER WARSHIPS AND AUXILIARIES IN JANUARY 1805					
Class	Guns	In commission	In ordinary	Building	Total
Bombs	8	17	0	0	17
Fire ships	14	1	0	0	1
Gun-brigs	10-14	83	0	7	83+7
Cutters	4-14	44	0	13	44+13
Gun-boats	1-4	5	0	0	5+0
Troop ships		14	7	0	21+0
Store ships		10	1	0	11+0
Advice boats		6	0	0	6+0

(Vessels on harbour service not shown)

waterline, which gave them a very shallow draught. This was useful for inshore work, but reduced internal volume. They were flush-decked and ship-rigged, with three masts.

Captain Schank's contributions included internal watertight bulkheads and the "sliding keel," a rectangular plate which could be lowered or raised vertically through a housing and slot in the kelson. These "sliding keels," made of wood with iron strengthening bands, were superficially similar to today's dagger-boards and one purpose was to prevent the vessel from sliding away to leeward. However, Schank's idea was more complex, since the two vessels had four "sliding keels" which were operated differentially to enhance control in various situations. The main (i.e., central) keels would normally be left lowered, except when running before the wind or in shallow water. To tack (go about) the stern keel was raised and the fore keel fully lowered, the helm put down, and then, as soon as the head was to the wind, the fore keel was raised again until the sails had filled, when it was once again lowered and left down. This, it was claimed, enabled the vessel to turn much faster than any other square-

rigged vessel, but also ensured that it would not "miss stays." When wearing (gybing) the procedure was to raise both fore and main keels, leaving only the stern keel down.

Reports on their performance varied, possibly according to whether the writer was receptive to new ideas, or not. Thus, *Arrow* was described as "stiff and a good sailor," while *Dart* was described as having "poor stability" and being "unsafe in a wind." Both vessels had successful operational careers, and it was generally accepted that they were fast and stable, but they were nevertheless always regarded as oddities and their design was not repeated.

Both vessels were initially armed with experimental guns, designed by Mr Sadler of the Admiralty Board of Works (the department headed by Bentham). These fired a 32-pounder shot, but were considerably shorter and lighter than the standard naval pieces (24cwt versus 55cwt) and recoiled on slides, a technique later used for carronades. These guns were unsatisfactory and were replaced by 28 32-pounder carronades, a very heavy armament for a vessel of this size.

HM Sloops
Arrow/Dart, **28**

Rating: Sloop

Guns: 28.

Construction: Redbridge, Thames.

Designer: Sir Samuel Bentham/Captain John Schank

Armament: Upper deck – 24 x 32lb carronade; quarterdeck – 2 x 32lb carronade; forecastle _ 2 x 32lb carronade.

Dimensions: Length of gundeck 124ft 8 in; beam 50ft 0in.

Tonnage: 386 tons.

Complement: 121

Ralph Detarison by Bunney Dodd.

R.Dodd inv. et sculp

ABOVE: Arrow and Dart (the prototypes for Jack Aubrey's Polychrest) were two 28-gun sloops built to the design of Sir Samuel Bentham. They had pointed bows and stern and dagger-boards, rather than a deep, fixed keel. In this action on the night of July 9/10 1800, Dart, Andromeda and some fireships attacked French shipping in Dunkirk roads. Dart carried the frigate La Desireé (40) in a daring attack; the French lost 100 killed and wounded out of 330, Dart had one killed and 10 wounded.

ARROW

Following commissioning in 1796, *Arrow* operated in home waters, mainly as a convoy escort, although in 1802 she was detached for anti-smuggling duties on the Devonshire coast. She was paid off briefly in early 1803 but then recommissioned and served as a convoy escort, but also including forays into the Mediterranean, Adriatic and Aegean seas. She carried out several successful cutting out operations and also survived a lightning strike without serious damage of injury. She was sent home for refit in 1804 and was back in the Mediterranean in early 1805.

In February 1805 she was escorting a large convoy, assisted by a bomb, when they were attacked by two large French frigates, *Hortense* (40) and *Incorruptible* (38). *Arrow* paid the price of her all-car-

ronade armament and was steadily reduced to a wreck by the French frigates' long guns. After an hour she was in a sinking condition, with 13 killed and 27 wounded, leaving her captain with no choice but to strike. In fact, she sank as her last people were being taken off, a most unusual event. Thanks to the sacrifice of *Arrow* and the bomb (which was captured shortly afterwards) only three ships in the convoy were lost.

DART

Like *Arrow*, *Dart* spent her first years operating in home waters. Her operations included a cutting out expedition on the Dutch coast in October 1799 and a fireship attack on frigates in Dunkirk roads in July 1800. In the latter, *Dart* was by far the most successful of the vessels involved and captured the French frigate *Desiree* (40) which lost 100 killed and wounded (out of 330) against *Dart*'s one killed and 11 wounded out of 121. *Dart* was also present at the Battle of Copenhagen (April 2, 1801). In 1805 she was sent to the West Indies, where her successes included capturing a privateer *Gabriella* (8). *Dart* returned to England and was decommissioned and broken up in 1808.

HMS *POLYCHREST*

These two vessels and their background have been described at some length, because there can be little doubt that these two sloops were the inspiration for Jack Aubrey's command, HMS *Polychrest*. The pointed stem and stern are strong indicators, as are the "top secret" trials of the Sadler guns, later removed.

Although, described as a "carpenter's mistake" they did, in fact, perform well in service and those prepared to come to terms with their idiosyncrasies obtained excellent performance from them. The clue may come in the word polychrest which is defined as "something adapted to several different uses; especially a drug or medicine serving to cure various diseases" since the Bentham/Schank design was also intended to overcome a variety of naval problems.

HMS *SPEEDY*

In the middle of the 18th century sloop designs started to increase in size, so a new type of vessel was developed—the brig—to replace them, the first being the Royal Navy's Childers-class. These measured some 200 tons and were armed with 10 4-pounders, later increased to 14. These brig-rigged, two-masters were fast and maneuverable, and were generally employed for dispatch work or as convoy escorts.

The most famous of the class was HMS *Speedy*, which was completed in 1782 and, following the outbreak of war in 1793, was employed on various duties on the Iberian coast and the western Mediterranean. This first part of her operational career ended off Nice on June 9, 1794 when her captain mistook three French frigates for the British squadron to which she was due to deliver dispatches and was too close to escape when he discovered his error. She was forced to surrender to greatly overpowering strength and was impressed into the French Navy, only to be recaptured by the British frigate, HMS *Inconstant* (36) in March 1795.

Following her recapture, *Speedy* remained in the Mediterranean and operated as part of a squadron off the coast of Italy which, for a period, was commanded by Commodore Horatio Nelson. In October 1799 *Speedy* attacked eight enemy

BELOW: Profile of Arrow *and* Dart, *prepared to Sir Samuel Bentham's design. Note the elegant design of the hull, with both ends pointed, the modern shape of the rudder, and the four dagger-boards. It was an integral part of Bentham's design that these boards were raised and lowered in various combinations according to the effect to be achieved. The system worked very well but was too advanced for the conservative officers of the Royal Navy.*

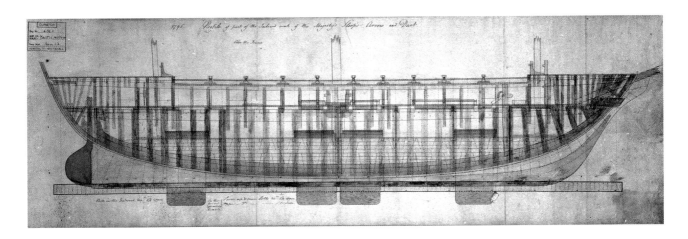

HMS *Speedy*

Rating: Brig.

Guns: 10 (later increased to 14).

Construction: King, Dover. Commissioned 1782.

Armament: 14 x 4-pounder.

Dimensions: Length 78ft 7in; beam 25ft 0in; draught 11ft 0in.

Tonnage: 202 tons.

Complement: 90.

merchant ships and a two-strong escort off Cape Trafalgar, six of which ran themselves ashore to avoid capture. In the following month she took on 12 Spanish gunboats escorting a transport carrying wine to the Spanish fleet and although she survived, Speedy suffered extensive damage and had to go to Gibraltar for repairs. In March 1800 she had a change of commanding officers, the new captain being Lieutenant Thomas Cochrane, heir to the Earl of Dundonald, thus beginning one of the most famous combinations of brig and captain in naval history, during which some 50 vessels were captured or destroyed; 534 prisoners were captured and 122 guns taken.

Cochrane exhibited remarkable impudence, a typical example occurring in December 1801, when Speedy was overtaken by a Spanish frigate sent to capture her. But one of Speedy's officers could speak Danish, so he hoisted the Danish national flag together with a quarantine pennant.

When the Spanish frigate was close enough the officer explained that they had just left a North African port and had plague aboard, which was sufficient to make any European ship of the day keep its distance and Cochrane was left unmolested.

Then, in a famous engagement on May 6, 1896, Speedy met the Spanish frigate El Gamo, armed with 22 12-pounders, eight 9-pounders, and two carronades, off the Spanish naval base of Barcelona. Cochrane was out-gunned (14 versus 32) and out-numbered (54 versus 319), and nobody could possibly have criticized him for keeping his distance, but he decided to attack. Showing tremendous panache, he ran in until he was alongside the larger ship and fired several treble-shotted broadsides into El Gamo, to which the Spaniards were unable to reply, since, as Cochrane had quickly appreciated, their guns were mounted too high to damage the smaller brig. Coming in even closer, the British brig

RIGHT: The brig HMS Speedy (14) built by King's of Dover and launched June 29, 1782. She was armed with fourteen 4-pounders and had a crew of 90. She is seen here ghosting up to some survivors from what appears to have been a much larger ship. From March 28, 1800 to 3 July 1801 Speedy was commanded by Lord Cochrane.

then grappled the larger Spanish frigate and Cochrane led a boarding party, which overcame the enemy in a short, sharp fight. The Spaniards lost 15 killed (including the captain) and 41 wounded, but British losses were much lighter, three dead and eight wounded. Cochrane and his men took *El Gamo* into Port Mahon, Minorca, although they had to train the main deck guns down the hatchways to ensure that their numerous captives did not try to retake the ship.

Cochrane's great valor earned him as many enemies in Whitehall as among the King's enemies and his reward for taking *El Gamo* was promotion to post-captain, but no more, and his first lieutenant was deliberately ignored. Then on July 3 *Speedy* was attacked by three French frigates and after a fierce resistance he was left with no choice but to haul down his flag. The senior French captain was so impressed that he declined to accept Cochrane's sword. The badly damaged *Speedy* was taken into port by her French captors, but what happened to her after that is not known.

HMS *NUTMEG OF CONSOLATION*

In his novel "Nutmeg of Consolation" Captain Jack Aubrey takes command of the former Dutch Navy sloop *Gelijkheid* (20) which had been sunk in local waters due to an outbreak of the plague. The vessel is renamed *Nutmeg of Consolation*. Unlike his other ships, no actual historical prototype can be found for this. There was a ship named *Gelijkheid* in the Dutch Navy, a 64-gun 3rd rate, which was captured at the Battle of Camperdown (October 11, 1797). She was then brought back to England, but she was hulked and employed as a prison ship from 1799 until broken up in 1814. It was Royal Navy practice for captured ships to retain their original names, unless there was a particular reason for not doing so; for

example, that there was already a ship of that name in the Royal Navy. But, as far as is known, this ex-Dutch ship's name was not changed during this period.

The Dutch built a series of sloops in the late 1790s and it is probable that they would have chosen names from earlier vessels, including those lost to the enemy. Judging by Dutch practice at the time the *Nutmeg of Consolation* is likely to have been brig-rigged (i.e., with two masts) and flush-decked, and like all Dutch designs would have been robust and fast. The historical *Gelijkheid* (64) was lost to the English at Camperdown and the fictional *Gelijkheid* (20) had to be sunk due to an outbreak of plague. It appears that Patrick O'Brien's choice of the name, which translates into English as "good fortune," was deliberately meant to be ironic.

HMS *Nutmeg of Consolation*

Rating: Sloop.

Guns: 20.

Construction: Netherlands

Armament: 20 x 8-pounder

Dimensions: Length 100ft 0in; beam 30ft 0in.

Tonnage: 300 tons.

Complement: 90.

[These specifications are speculative; see notes in text.]

LEFT: Captain Lord Thomas Cochrane (1775-1860), later 10th Earl of Dundonald, one of whose appointments was as commanding officer of HMS Speedy (14). One of the most daring, imaginative and intrepid officers of his day, Cochrane was popular with his crew and fellow officers, but not with his superiors and the Admiralty, whom he was more than ready to criticize if he felt that they were at fault.

CHAPTER III

SAILS AND SAILING

Sailing warships were the most complex machines in existence and sailors extremely skilled in their use, but even so they were utterly dependant on natural phenomena over which they had no control and limited understanding; namely the strength and direction of the wind, the tides and ocean currents. Thus ships could be prevented from leaving harbour for days, perhaps weeks, and even when at sea they were often forced to approach their objective in an oblique manner or in a series of

KEY
1. Flying jib
2. Jib.
3. Fore topmast staysail.
4. Fore staysail.
5. Foresail/forecourse.
6. Fore topsail.
7. Fore topgallant.
8. Mainstaysail.
9. Main topmast staysail.
10. Middle staysail.
11. Main topgallant staysail.
12. Mainsail/course.
13. Main topsail.
14. Main topgallant sail.
15. Mizen staysail.
16. Mizen topmast staysail.
17. Mizen topgallant staysail.
18. Mizen sail.
19. Spanker/driver.
20. Mizen topsail.
21. Mizen topgallant.

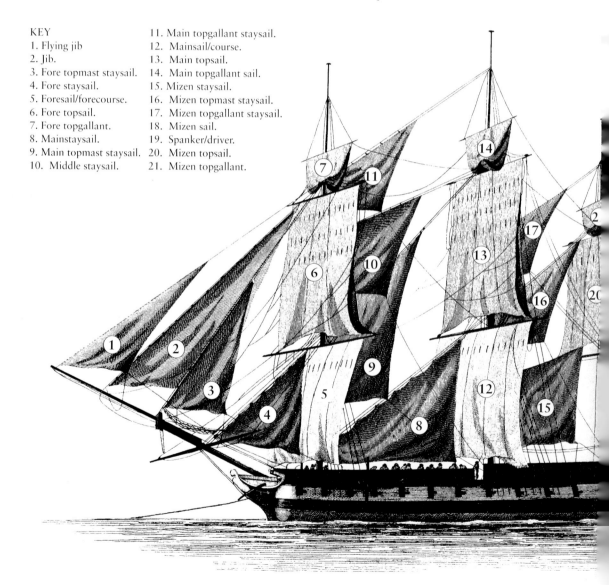

RIGHT: HMS Cambrian *(40) with her principle sails hung out to dry to enable them to be identified.*

Notes.
A. Certain parts of the rigging have been omitted for clarity.
B. Studding sails and booms, and the spritsail have been omitted.
C. Either the mizen or the spanker would be set, not both.

dog-legs, while on other occasions they found themselves drifting helplessly in a total calm. In addition, the sea was a hard taskmaster and storms, tempests, uncharted rocks and a hostile shore all took their toll. Indeed, as shown in the table on page 42 overleaf, the losses during the wars due to accidental causes were far more severe than those inflicted by the enemy:

RIGS

The standing rigging comprised a complex combination of masts, spars and ropes, strong enough to stand on its own and to withstand the shocks of weather and battle, but without being so heavy that it unbalanced the vessel, a condition sailors termed

ABOVE: HMS Thetis *(38) has run aground on the North Carolina coast in 1794. Three anchors have been deployed, two from the stern and one from the port bow, to try to warp her off. It took a week of backbreaking work, but they succeeded in the end.*

BRITISH WARSHIP LOSSES FEBRUARY 1793 – JULY 1815						
Vessels (see note)	Combat Losses		Accidental Losses			Total
	Sunk	Captured	Wrecked	Foundered	Fire	
Line	0	5	17	3	8	33
Others	16	120	234	72	7	349
TOTALS	16	125	251	75	15	382

Note: "Others" includes vessels from frigates down to brigs, but excludes cutters, advice ships and other very small craft.

"crank." The sails were of two main types. "Square sails" were suspended from yards and deployed athwartships, although only a few, such as the courses, were truly rectangular in shape, virtually all the others being wider at the bottom than the top. "Fore-and-aft" sails were on the centreline and suspended from a stay, except for the spanker which was suspended from a gaff. Every one of these sails had a unique name,

RIGHT: An English frigate in distress in the Bay of Biscay, unable to hoist even a stormsail or a reefed sail. Her status is confirmed by the national flag being flown upside down.

derived from the mast or stay they were on and their position. This multiplicity of sails was designed to give the captain and the master the means to optimize the vessel's performance in the light of the frequently changing conditions.

Masts

When a vessel had only one mast it was called the mainmast. In a two-masted vessel they were named according to their size and position; if the forward mast was the taller it was called the mainmast and the other the mizen (the spelling was changed to mizzen in the 20th century), but if the after mast was the taller then that was the mainmast, the other the foremast.

Each mast consisted of up to four sections, named in ascending order: lower mast, topmast, topgallant mast and royalmast. The lower mast passed down through holes in the deck known as partners and was stepped on the kelson. Masts were held in position by forestays which extended forward on the centerline of the vessel, while there were two sets of backstays extending aft to be secured to the sides by channel plates. The masts were stayed athwartships by shrouds.

In smaller vessels, the mast was made of a single piece of timber, but in larger vessels the required length and diameter were so great that the mast was assembled from a number of sections doweled and glued together, pinned using iron nails and finally

LEFT: Frigate running before the wind. The spritsail is set but no jibs, and the fore- and foretopmast-studding sails are set on the starboard side only, to avoid masking.

bound by lengths of rope known as woldings or, as became the increasing practice from the early years of the 19th century, iron bands.

For many years prior to the War of American Independence the Royal Navy's masts were made of New England white pine, but when this source ended in 1776 the only suitable alternative was a similar white pine from Riga (in modern Latvia). This need for timber was one of the main reasons the British were so keen on keeping the Baltic open to trade.

BELOW: Ship's bow showing the sharp upward angle of the bowsprit. Note the gammoning, some 12 turns of rope bracing the bowsprit down against the lift of the stays.

Bowsprit

The bowsprit extended forward of the bows and was regarded as a mast, and, also like a mast, it had an extension—the jib-boom. The bowsprit was usually angled upwards, sometimes as much as 25 degrees, and posed some fascinating engineering problems, since it took considerable strain from various stays that were anchored to it. These included the forestay and foretop-

mast stay, which all tended to lift the bowsprit and jibboom upwards, the strain being increased yet further when the various jibs were deployed.

The first step in overcoming this was that just outboard of where the bowsprit emerged from the hull it was braced downwards by some eight to twelve turns of rope which passed over the sprit and then down and through a slot in the cutwater; an arrangement known as gammoning. In addition to this a short boom known as the dolphin striker extended downwards from the bowsprit cap and was used to anchor the martingale stays, of which most warships normally had two. There were also two yards, one suspended from the bowsprit, the other from the jib-boom.

Yards

Yards were long cylindrical pieces of fir timber suspended from the mast, whose purpose was to extend the sails to catch the wind. Such yards were either "square", i.e. suspended at right angles to the mast, or "lateen" in which case they were suspended obliquely at one-third their length. As was normal practice among naval architects of that era, the sizes were calculated on a proportional basis; for example, the mainyard was usually eight-ninths the length of the main mast and the foreyard seven-eighths of the length of the mainyard, and so on. The diameter of the yards at their mid-point was calculated in a similar manner, that for the main and foreyards being one-quarter of an inch for every foot of their length. In warships the main and foreyards were usually made up of different pieces scarfed together, the others being single pieces of timber. The mid-section of the yard was octagonal in cross-section and of constant thickness, while the outer parts were circular and tapered to a point.

The yard was hoisted into position by ropes known as jeers and then held in place by an arrangement of ropes known as parrels, which enabled the angle of the yard to be adjusted. The angle relative to the horizontal was set by two ropes known as lifts, which were secured at the masthead and then ran through pulleys at the yard arm, back up to the masthead, through a second pulley and then down to the deck, where they could be adjusted. Braces ran from each yardarm down to the deck where they were used to adjust the angle relative to the centreline to make maximum use of the wind.

Hanging below every yard were a num-

LEFT: The topmast area. Below is the main top (note the "lubber's hole") and doubling. Above that is topsail yard, with a complicated array of lifts and braces; at the top are the topmast crosstrees and doubling.

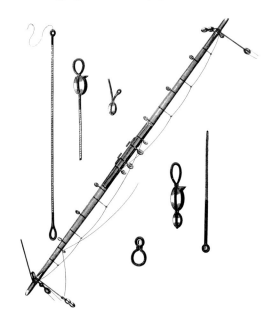

LEFT: A yard, from which a squaresail was suspended. Note the stirrups enabling the crew to move along the yard and also to serve as a brace when hands were involved with the sail.

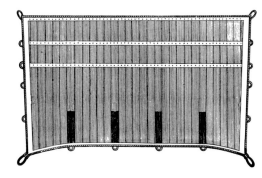

LEFT: British sails were made from strips of stout canvas, 2 feet wide, in various strengths: No 1 (strongest) to No 8 (weakest). The boltrope runs around the entire outer edge of the sail.

SQUARE SAILS IN THEIR RELATIVE POSITIONS				
Masthead		Fore Topgallant Royal	Main Topgallant Royal	Mizen Topgallant Royal
↑		Fore Topgallant*	Main Topgallant*	Mizen Topgallant
	Spritsail Topsail	Fore Topsail*	Main topsail*	Mizen Topsail
	Spritsail	Foresail*	Mainsail*	
	Bowsprit	Foremast	Mainmast	Mizen Mast
↓				
Deck	Bow ←			→ Stern

*(Sails marked * could be extended by the addition of studding sails)*

FORE-AND-AFT SAILS IN THEIR RELATIVE POSITIONS							
Masthead ↑ ↓ Deck	Jib	Fore Topmast Staysail	For Staysail	Main Topgallant Staysail	Mizen Topgallant Staysail	
				Middle Staysail		
				Main Topmast Staysail	Mizen Topmast Staysail	
				Main Staysal	Mizen Staysail	Driver/Spanker
				Between Foremast and Mainmast	Between Mainmast and Mizen	Mizen
				←Bow		Stern→

(Note that all were bent to stays except for the Driver/Spanker)

RIGHT: A small selection of sails. The outer, or flying jib (near right); mizen topgallant staysail (far right top); mizen staysail; (far right center) and a loose-footed mizen (far right lower).

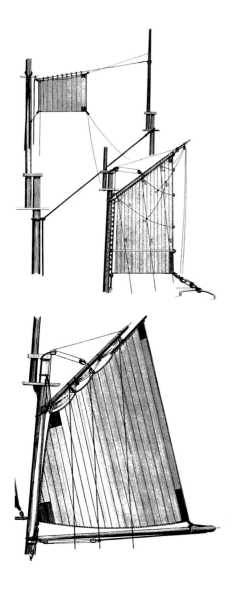

ber of stirrups ending in an eye, through which passed a rope known as the horse, which provided a continuous walk-way for the topmen. It was most important that the horses were moused (i.e., secured) to each stirrup to provide a stable foothold, since otherwise a heavy man would depress his section forcing lighter men upwards.

Sails had a language all their own. They were bent (i.e., secured) to yards, booms or gaffs, spread when making sail, furled when reducing sail, and, in certain cases, reduced in area in stormy weather by a process known as reefing. The top edge of a square-sail was the head, the bottom the foot, the sides the leeches, and the corner between the foot and the leach was a clew.

The names of the squaresails identified which mast they were on and their position on that mast—see table opposite. The main, top and topgallant sails could be extended in light weather by the addition of studding sails (stuns'ls) which were suspended from special booms run out from the appropriate yard. The majority of the fore-and-aft sails were bent to stays (part of the standing rigging) and took their names from the relevant stay, except for the driver (also known as the spanker) which was bent to the mizen. All sails were made of strips of stout canvas, which in the British case were a standard two feet wide, and their strength varied from No 1 (strongest) to No 8 (weakest). Sails were edged all round by a boltrope.

Working Aloft

Shrouds gave lateral support to the masts and were linked by horizontal ropes called ratlines to form a ladder, which the sailors used to ascend the masts to work on the sails or rigging. The shrouds took them as far as a platform known as a top, which could be entered either by going round the outside using the futtock (foothook) shrouds or directly through a gap, designed specifically for that purpose. A second set of shrouds took them up to the next level. Once at the required level the sailor would then transfer to the yard using the horse (footrope), with his arms over the yard.

Working aloft was inherently dangerous even in calm weather, and infinitely more so in heavy weather when the topmen were

not only coping with the elements but also having to struggle with heavy, flapping sails or heavy booms with an apparent will of their own. Captains took a pride in the crew's performance aloft and the vast majority of sailors also enjoyed demonstrating their prowess. Men would race up the ratlines and then go round the outside of the top on the futtock shrouds, since the much easier and safer method of going through the gap was considered (to use a modern phrase) "chicken," as indicated by the disparaging name, the "lubbers' hole." Younger midshipmen would egg each other

BELOW: Reefing sails was a hazardous job, only taking place in strong winds when the large sails were flapping with considerable power.

RIGHT: Heaving-to (i.e.,
stopping in the water) by
backing the foresails.

on, often with bets, to perform feats of daring such as running along the yards rather than sidling along the footropes and all would descend in virtual free-fall down the stays rather than clamber down the ratlines. Losses aloft were not unusual and if he lost his footing the more fortunate sailor would fall outboard, where he had a small chance of being rescued by a boat, whereas falling to the deck was almost certain death.

Reefing was a particularly arduous func-

tion, not least because it took place as the weather worsened. Unwanted sails were first hauled down; e.g., the studding sails, royals, and topgallants, together with the staysails, all of which were intended for light winds and had no reefing points. Next it was necessary to spill the wind from the sail, which was achieved by hauling on the clew lines and rounding in the weather brace. At this point the men deployed along the yard, all standing on the horse except for the outer man on the weather side who sat astride the yard and started to pull on the earring, the other men assisting by leaning over the yard, grabbing a reefing point and pulling the sail towards the weather side. As soon as the man had secured the weather end of the sail the man at the other end of the yard secured the lee-

RIGHT: Ship getting under
way, with hands at the
yards freeing the sails.

LEFT: Heaving-to using topsails only, with main topsail backed only.

ward end and all then grabbed the front and rear reefing points and tied them with a reef knot. This took in the first reef, but had to be repeated if the captain or master ordered further reefs to be taken in.

The spritsail was bent to the spritsail yard, which was suspended underneath the bowsprit. It was one of the few square sails in the vessel and had an unusual feature, in that because it was usually immersed in water, there were two drainage holes stitched into each side near the foot to prevent the bag of the sail from becoming waterlogged.

Weights

One of the most frequent activities aboard a warship was the raising and lowering of heavy objects, such as masts, yards, cannon, ship's boats, water casks and wet sails. The crews were very skilful at employing the limited means available to them, although since the most frequent physical complaint recorded by ship's doctors were hernias it would seem that they were not always successful. In harbour, a sheer-hulk was usually available, but away from such resources the crew had to make their own arrangements, as was frequently the case following damage in battle or by a storm.

Crews were exceptionally adept at solving mechanical problems, especially when a task seized their imagination, such as the occupation of the island called Diamond Rock in 1803. To establish their gun battery ashore they lifted two guns some 700 feet to the top of the rock direct from their ship and also sent cannon and ammunition to the beach, where they were raised using a device they nicknamed the "stage coach." These prodigious feats were achieved using a combination of equipment available aboard their ship, muscle power and imagination.

Sailing

The officers and sailors of the time were undoubtedly extremely skilled at making the best use of the ships and rigging at their disposal but, unfortunately for them, the

RIGHT: Frigate getting
under way, with sails set
and about to be sheeted
home.

BELOW: In a strong wind
under reduced sail
(staysails only) to
maintain steerage way.

warships of the period were not particularly good designs. A sailing ship's ability was assessed by its ability to sail close to the wind, which was expressed in terms of "points," each compass point equalling 11 degrees 15 minutes. Experience showed that a square-rigged ship when sailing close-hauled (i.e., as close to the wind as possible) could not lie better than six points. This meant that if the wind was from due north the nearest course a ship could sail was east north-east (63 degrees 45 minutes). Performance was also affected by the length and shape of the hull, and by the extent to which the hull was fouled by marine growths. Poor hull design also meant that, except when running before the wind, ships fell away to leeward, the rate depending upon a combination of hull design and the strength of the wind. All these shortcomings were, of course, understood by the mariners of the time and they employed their experience and skills to alleviate them.

The combination of a multiplicity of sails, both square and fore-and-aft, and the means to control each of them through braces, tacks, bowlines and sheets enabled captains and masters to use them both individually and collectively to the best advantage. Thus, when sailing on a constant course, the necessary sails would be set, ensuring that all were pulling properly and

none was masking another, and, if they were, they were either furled or lowered. Further, when changing course to tack or wear, some sails could be drawing, some allowed to flap and others even deliberately set aback in order to achieve the best result as quickly as possible.

Mistakes were punished almost instantly and expensively, and could easily result in a broken spar or a ripped sail. However, one of the worst errors was to "miss stays," due to a miscalculation by the master or bad performance by the crew. This meant that the ship failed to go about and left no option but to pay off back onto the previous course and build up speed in order to try again. At the best of times this was an embarrassing inconvenience, but in the middle of a battle it could result in a major tactical setback.

LEFT: Two-decker with the wind on the quarter.

BELOW: A 5th Rate lying-to in a heavy sea, in order to allow the storm-tossed rowing boat and its laboring crew to come alongside.

CHAPTER IV

NAVAL WEAPONS

It is extraordinary that from the reign of Henry VIII to the time of the Napoleonic Wars there was no fundamental change in the principle of gun design, which continued to be a simple metal tube, with a charge and round ball rammed in from the muzzle, and the charge ignited by a fuse running through a vent at the rear. Of course, there were some advances, but even the pressures of the 23-year war against France saw only a few refinements in naval gunnery, rather the succession of technological revolutions spurred by much shorter 20th century wars. There were a number of experimental designs such as the Sadler guns tested in *Arrow* (see Chapter Two), but even this and the carronade were essentially variations on the closed tube theme.

The only major advances in cannon tech-

RIGHT: Gun crew in action. This required the greatest degree of teamwork if it was to be done both efficiently and safely, since any error could resulted in injury or death. Gun crews were usually reinforced by the members from the opposite gun, it is was not engaged.

nology took place in the 1780s when the material was changed from brass to iron, enabling them to be cast solid and then bored out, resulting in stronger and safer barrels. The cast barrel was also more accurate, although it was not until the early 1800s that rudimentary sights began to be fitted.

Many Royal Navy admirals and captains considered gunnery to be an art and, unlike their land-based colleagues in the Royal Artillery, few gave much thought to scientific aspects and ballistics; indeed, even the ship's warrant officer gunners had little technical knowledge. Where gunnery was concerned, what was really important to most naval officers was gun drill; i.e., the rapidity with which the guns could be handled and fired. Indeed, naval tactics were geared to the gun rather than vice versa and in general terms the Royal Navy's prime requirement was to close very rapidly with an enemy, and then inflict as much damage as possible using rapid fire at extremely close range—many reports of engagements describe guns being fired at pistol range (i.e., about 15 yards)—and then finishing off by boarding.

Apart from the implicit hazard in storing and handling gunpowder, the major danger was the violent recoil, which not only meant that gun crews had to stand well clear as the weapon was fired, but also that

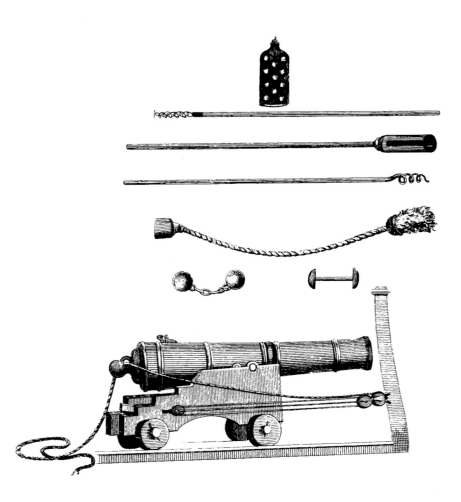

the gun carriage had somehow to be controlled and the forces dissipated. This was achieved by mounting the gun on a very substantial wooden carriage, usually made from elm, which was mounted on four trucks and restrained by ropes secured to the ship's side. It was essential that this tackle operated smoothly and it had to be kept untangled, even at the height of a battle.

Guns

The number and type of guns in the design of a ship was laid down by the Admiralty in the "Establishment" and then became the basis for its "rating" as discussed in Chapter

ABOVE: The basic design of long cannon and carriages did not change for several centuries, although this particular weapon has a gun-lock, similar to that used on muskets. Above are various types of shot and cleaning tools.

ABOVE: The gun-deck of
HMS Bellerophon (74).
Here all is calm and tidy,
but in battle it would be
crowded, full of smoke,
and noisy beyond modern
comprehension.

One. The further complication, also discussed in Chapter One, was that only long cannon counted; carronades were simply ignored.

Carronades

General Robert Melville invented a new type of cannon in 1752, which was manufactured at the Carron Iron Works from 1779 onwards, giving rise to its name—the carronade. In essence, this was a short-barreled gun using a smaller powder charge to fire a heavy (32 or 64lb) ball with a low muzzle velocity, which had a crushing and splintering effect far greater than that of a high velocity ball at the short ranges for which it was designed.

Early carronades had mid-mounted trunnions on the same type of carriage as a gun, but this was changed to two lugs beneath the barrel, attached to a bed, with a worm screw at the breech for elevation. This bed sat atop a platform and the recoil was absorbed by friction. The entire carriage was raised clear of the deck and pivoted on a vertical bolt at the front and two small trucks at the rear, enabling the weapon to be traversed. All this meant that the carronade required a much smaller crew than a conventional gun.

The carronade was adopted by the Royal Navy during the American War of Independence, and thereafter was used as the main quarterdeck deck weapon in frigates and as the major weapon in sloops and brigs. It gave these smaller ships a devastating broadside at very close range, but during the War of 1812 carronades were found to be less useful in single-ship engagements, since American ships could sit outside carronade range and just pound away. So by 1814-15 carronades were omitted from new designs and replaced by long guns.

Other Guns

Apart from the carronade, a number of different gun designs appeared during the war, but all were variations on the nuzzle-loading, closed-tube theme. A battery of 32-pounders designed by a Mr Sadler of the Naval Works Department was tested aboard the experimental sloops *Arrow* and *Dart*, but they were soon removed and replaced by carronades. Another design was produced by Captain Gover and his 24-pounders were mounted aboard some ships in the mid-years of the war, but did not find general favor. The most successful was the Congreve gun, designed by the inventor of the rocket system, which was essentially a compromise between the traditional long gun and the carronade, being shorter and fatter than the former but with a better range and recoil system than the latter; it was mounted in a number of frigates in 1814-15.

Firing

Although a broadside (i.e., all guns on one side firing simultaneously) was potentially devastating to the enemy, it also imposed a tremendous strain on the structure of the parent ship. In practice, other modes of firing were more usual, including firing in nominated groups, by quarters, by deck, in succession, "fire as you bear" and "independent firing," the latter two being totally at the discretion of the gun captains. There were, of course, some innovators, such as Captain Sir Charles Douglas, who invented a device to enable gun captains to fire their guns at an angle, but this placed an uneven

BELOW: The short-barrelled carronade fired a heavy ball over a relatively short range. In the Royal Navy such carronades did not count when assessing a ship's rating, which was based solely on the number of long cannon.

PERFORMANCE OF SELECTED ENGLISH GUNS				
	32-pounder long gun	32-pounder carronade	Congreve 24-pounder	Remarks
Calibre	6.4in	6.3in	5.8in	Internal diameter of barrel
Weight of barrel	2.8 tons	0.9 tons	2.1 tons	Barrel, but less carriage
Length of barrel	10ft 0in	4ft 0in	7ft 6in	From muzzle to button
Maximum range	3000yd at 10°	1,000yd at 5°	1,500yd at 5°	Elevation limited by gun port and carriage design
Effective range	350yd	330yd	580yd	Point blank; i.e., at 0° elevation

strain on the tackles, which then tended to self-center the gun as it fired, thus negating the effect of aiming.

Firing sequence

Firing a gun followed a set pattern:
- Gun fired.
- Gun ran back to the extent permitted by the tackle.
- The sponge on the end of the ramrod was dipped in water and pushed down the barrel until it reached the chamber. It was then twisted in order to douse and remove any burning or smoldering remnants from the previous cartridge. The ramrod was then removed, and the sponge shaken and tapped against the barrel to remove any grit.
- The new cartridge was removed from its wooden/metal container and placed inside the muzzle, followed by a wad.
- At the same time the gun captain placed the priming wire in the vent and held it there.
- The cartridge and first wad were pushed down the barrel by the ramrod until the captain felt the cartridge touch the priming wire and he called out "home."
- The gun captain used the priming wire to prick open the cartridge, then removed it.

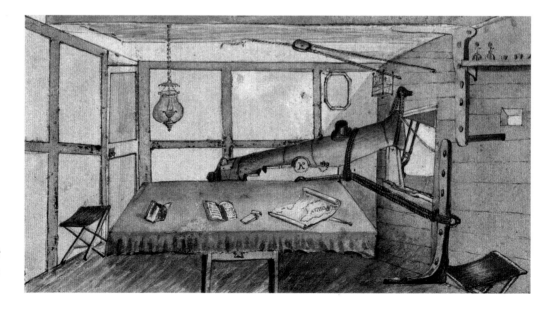

RIGHT: An officer's cabin aboard HMS Gloucester, which he shared with one of the cannon. Note the lashings, which held the cannon rigidly locked in place when not in use.

- The rammer was removed and the round and a second wad placed in muzzle and rammed home.
- The gun was run out; this was the single most manpower-intensive task and involved the entire gun team.
- The gun captain inserted the quill tube in the vent and cocked the gunlock.
- The gun was aimed using the quoin for elevation and handspike to alter the training angle.
- The crew stood well clear and the gun captain pulled the lanyard.
- The gun fired and recoiled, and the sequence restarted.

Gun crew

The actual number of a gun's crew depended upon the gun's size, a rule-of-thumb employed at the time being that one man was required for every 5cwt (deadweight) of gun; thus, a 32-pounder had a crew of 7 and an 18-pounder a crew of 6. But, selected men in most gun-crews had alternative tasks which, if called for, they had no choice but to leave to perform. These included such duties as forming a boarding party, operating the pump, trimming the sails or damage control. Not all would be called for simultaneously, but the position was alleviated somewhat because if only one side of the ship was engaged, as was the norm, the men from the disengaged side joined them, thus effectively doubling the gun crew. When this was done the gun captain of the engaged side's gun was in charge, the gun captain of the other gun his second-in-command, and so on.

There was discussion from time to time concerning the fact that the men in the shore-based Royal Artillery gun crews were told off by numbers, with each individual "gun number" having a specific and well understood task. The navy resisted this on the grounds that while a shore-based gun crew remained constant (except, of course, if there were casualties), the numbers in a naval crew varied in an unpredictable fashion throughout an engagement.

Because range and accuracy were so poor the Royal Navy depended upon closing rapidly with the enemy and then simply slogging it out, firing directly into the enemy's hull (unlike the French, who deliberately fired at the enemy's rigging. This British practice was partly because they always tried to obtain the weather gage, which meant that the engaged side was heeling

BELOW: Captain Sir Philip Broke of HMS Shannon. Broke trained his guncrews to a high degree of proficiency and devised many aids to improve their accuracy and rate of fire.

slightly towards the enemy, anyway, and also because even with flintlocks the firing process was slow, so that the gunner tended to fire as the ship commenced its downward roll.

Not many statistics survive but a great gun under independent control and with its full crew present was probably capable of firing one round per minute. Range of the 32-pounder was taken to be about one nautical mile and some crews may have been able to fire with some degree of accuracy at such a range, but the Royal Navy's general tactic was to get as close as possible and some engagements took place at "pistol range" or even less.

There were, however, some RN captains who took gunnery very seriously, a prime example being Captain Sir Philip Broke of HMS *Shannon*, 38. His gun crews were not only very highly trained, but they also had numerous aids (many devised by Broke himself) including gunsights, carriages adjusted to take account of the slant of the deck both athwartships and longitudinally (which suggests that he had appreciated the effect of trunnion tilt), and instruments to assess the range. As a result, when she met

USS *Chesapeake* on June 1 1813, *Shannon*'s gunners destroyed the American vessel in a little over five minutes by their deadly and highly accurate shooting. It was a salutary lesson that gunnery was not just a matter of drills.

Ammunition

There were various types of ammunition, the basic round being a solid iron ball. There was also a variety of anti-personnel rounds such as "canister," which consisted of a large number of small shot in a canvas or light metal container, and langrel which was similar but filled with scrap iron; both were highly effective, but only at very short range.

There were also anti-rigging rounds, intended to dismast enemy ships or at least to damage their rigging; these consisted of either two balls linked by a chain, or an extending bar. The number of rounds to be carried at the start of a voyage was laid down in the Board of Ordnance regulations, typical outloads per gun for a ship-of-the-line being: solid shot—80; dismantling shot—3 and grape shot—5.

BELOW: Launching Congreve rockets from a longboat, using a ladder as the launching ramp. The crew is a mixture of sailors to man the boat and men of the Royal Artillery for the rockets.

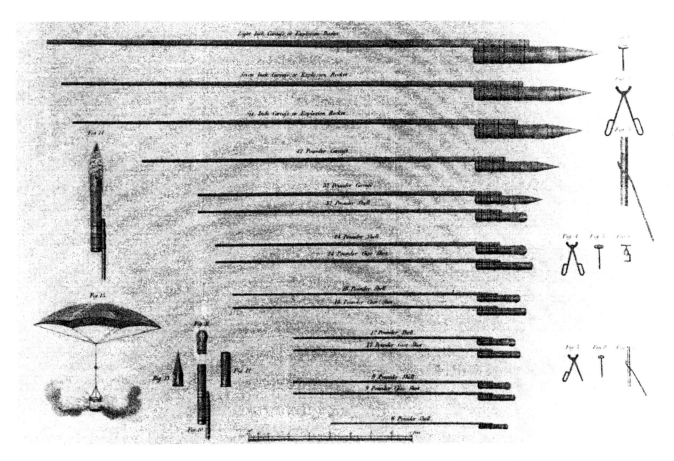

Propellant

Gunpowder was a highly dangerous mixture of saltpeter (potassium nitrate), sulphur and charcoal, which was stored in the powder-room (magazine), with special protection and under the supervision of the Yeoman of the Powder Room. The powder charges were contained in flannel bags and were delivered to the guns by young, agile boys known as "powder monkeys."

Rockets

The rocket was invented in China and also used in India, and was developed in the West by Sir William Congreve, a prolific English inventor, who worked for the Board of Ordnance. The Congreve rocket was a very simple device consisting of a metal cylinder containing the propellant and war-head and which had a pointed front-end, and a stabilizing stick. Various warheads could be installed, including explosive, incendiary (known as "carcass") and shrapnel, as well as an illuminating flare, whose effect was enhanced by a parachute. The rockets were normally classified by their weight, the most common being 32- and 42-pounders, although the largest were classified by the diameter of the cylinder – 6-, 7- and 8-inches. The most commonly used at sea was the 32-pounder which had a range of about 3,500 yards, but all were inherently inaccurate and could only be used against area targets.

The 32-pounder rocket consisted of an iron cylinder 42 inches long and four inches in diameter, with a screw-on conical nose covering. The stabilizing stick was strapped to the side of the body and was 15 feet long. The rockets were usually fired from a

ABOVE: The complete range of Congreve rockets, war-heads and tools. The parachute illuminating flare presaged a wide range of long-life flares still in use today.

National Designation	England/USA		Denmark		Dutch		French		Spain		Sweden		Russia	
	lb	oz	lb	oz	lb	oz	lb	oz	lb	oz	lb	oz	lb	oz
48-pdr											45	0		
42-pdr											39	6	37	14
36-pdr			39	12			38	14	36	8	33	12	32	8
32-pdr	32	0			34	13								
30-pdr											28	2	27	10
24-pdr	24	0	26	8	26	2	25	15	24	6	22	8	21	11
18-pdr	18	0	19	14	19	10	19	7	18	4	16	14	16	4
12-pdr	12	0	13	4	13	1	12	15	12	3	11	4	10	13
8-pdr	8	0	8	13	8	11	8	10	8	2	7	8	7	3
6-pdr	6	0	6	9	6	9	6	8	6	1	5	10	5	7

GUN DESIGNATIONS OF MAJOR NAVIES 1792-1815 AND THEIR EQUIVALENTS IN ENGLISH/US WEIGHTS

[Note that in the English/US system, 16 ounces (oz) = 1 pound (lb)]

"bombarding frame" consisting of a 15-foot long shallow trough, supported by two 12 foot poles, which could be mounted on the deck of a ship or in an open boat. A more permanent mounting was also devised in which a number of troughs were mounted at an angle in the hull, with the exit hole at about the same level as the gun ports. One bomb, HMS *Erebus*, received such a major conversion, and was employed during the War of 1812.

The "Pounder" Anomaly

During these wars the eight major navies identified their cannon by the weight of a solid shot fired by that weapon, expressed in pounds. However, because of their joint history England and the United States shared a common standard, but the other six nations defined the pound weight slightly differently, with the results shown in the table above.

This meant that, to take the example of three nations firing a nominal 24-pounder shot, the English/American shot weighed 24 pounds, but the Dutch shot weighed 26lb 8oz (in English measurement), while a Russian 24-pounder shot weighed rather less at 21lb 11oz.

To complicate the issue further, what the Danes described as a 36-pounder actually weighed more than a Russian or Swedish 42-pounder.

RIGHT: Royal Navy Officer's Sea Service sword; length about 30 inches. This was a very practical weapon, which was frequently required for use in hand-to-hand combat at sea.

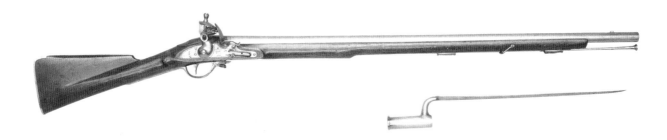

Handguns

All warships carried handguns, predominantly muskets and pistols made at the Board of Ordnance's arsenal at the Tower of London or by contractors. The "Short Sea Service Musket" was 46 inches long, weighed 9lb 4oz, and fired a 0.75 inch diameter ball. Being unrifled accuracy was not great and effective range was of the order of 100 yards, although a trained marksman might achieve slightly more.

All Royal Marine corporals and privates carried a musket and there was also a number for issue to sailors for shore operations or on boarding parties. Pistols were also

always held and issued in pairs. A stock of hand grenades was also carried. All these weapons were under the charge of the gunner.

Edged Weapons

Officers and midshipmen had their own swords. The officers sword was to a standard design with a 30 inch blade, while midshipmen had a much shorter weapon known as a dirk, with an 18 inch blade. The gunner also held a large stock of cutlasses for issue to boarding parties, together with a miscellany of other weapons, including pikes, axes and tomahawks.

ABOVE: The short Sea Service Musket with its bayonet was 46 inches long and weighed 9lb 4oz. Accuracy was poor and maximum effective range was of the order of 100 yards.

BELOW: Midshipman's dirk, with an 18 inch blade. Midshipmen could be as young as 12 year's old, but took part in hand-to-hand fighting and needed a light weapon such as this.

CHAPTER V

UNIFORMS 1795-1815

BELOW LEFT: Admiral in 1795-1812 pattern full dress, wearing the sash of the Order of the Bath.

BELOW RIGHT: Nelson's Trafalgar uniform, with Turkish chelengk in his hat and green eye-patch.

The first standard naval dress was introduced in 1748, but only for officers. The Admiralty then allowed only minor changes over the next 40 years until a new officers' pattern was introduced in 1787. This was being worn in 1793 when the war against revolutionary France began, but there was a second major change in 1795 and another in 1812. The first of these, in 1795, seems to have been due to a combination of the current simplification of civilian dress, combined with a desire to reduce unnecessary expense in wartime. The changes in 1812 were due mainly to the influence of the Prince of Wales, whose accession to Prince Regent in 1811 enabled him to put his wishes on Army and Navy uniforms into effect.

Naval officers had two official orders of dress: "full dress" for formal events and "undress" for all other occasions. The latter was normally worn at sea, although even less formal and more serviceable attire was necessary in bad or cold weather. But, even when all officers were wearing the same order of dress, they were by no means

always dressed identically. This was partly due to the wearer's financial situation—waistcoats or stockings of better quality, for example—but personal idiosyncrasies also played a part, which has always been a failing among certain types of British officer for whom the very word "uniform" seems to be a personal challenge. Also, individual ships sometimes adopted a particular embellishment, while officers on long overseas cruises—some of which lasted two years or more—might be unaware of changes until they returned.

The uniforms and embellishments were designed to indicate two things: first, that the wearer was a Royal Navy officer and secondly his rank. The Royal Navy aspect was covered by a general similarity of uniforms, which consisted of a black cocked hat, "navy" blue coat, white waistcoat,

breeches and stockings, and black buckled shoes, combined with a distinctive, naval-pattern sword.

The 1795 pattern full dress fell into three categories: admirals; captains and commanders; and lieutenants. All grades of admiral wore the same basic uniform. The coat (known as a "frock") had a stand-up, gold-fringed collar, long lapels also edged with gold braid and with nine buttons, each with a strip of horizontal braid. The rank of the wearer was indicated in two ways. All wore two identical epaulettes (shoulder-boards with gold bullion fringes) but with different numbers of embroidered stars: rear-admiral wore one; a vice-admiral two and an admiral three. The cuffs all had a horizontal broad golden stripe with three buttons and button-holes with vertical braided stripes, together with narrower

ABOVE LEFT: Captain, full dress, 1795-1812 pattern. The hat is being worn "fore-and-aft."

ABOVE RIGHT: Captain, undress, 1795-1812 pattern. This time the hat is of the "athwartships" style.

ABOVE LEFT: *Full dress for a Commander (1795-1812), as for a post-captain but with only one epaulette.*

ABOVE RIGHT: *Undress for a Lieutenant, 1787-1812. Note white piping and stand-up collar.*

horizontal stripes; again, a rear-admiral wore one, a vice-admiral two, and an admiral three.

Full dress for captains and commanders was generally similar to that of admirals, but with minor differences, the first being that the lapel buttons did not have the horizontal gold braids. Secondly, there was a turned back cuff, lined with gold braid and with three vertically-aligned buttons, and with two horizontal stripes underneath. The epaulettes were similar to those of admirals, but without the stars: commanders had one on left shoulder; a captain, on promotion, wore one on right shoulder, and a captain with over three years in the rank wore one on each shoulder. The lieutenant's coat had white lapels with nine buttons, white turned back cuffs with three buttons,

a plain blue collar and no epaulettes.

Undress was much simpler. Virtually all gold braid was omitted and no epaulettes were worn. From admiral down to commander the coat had a plain lapel, decorated only with nine buttons, and a plain stand-up collar. Rank was designated only on the cuff: all had three buttons in a horizontal row, admirals had three rows of horizontal braid, vice-admirals two and rear-admirals one; captains and commanders had just the three buttons and no gold braid. Lieutenants' lapels had nine buttons and were lined with narrow white piping and the collar was also piped in white. The cuffs had three horizontal buttons with the same type of narrow white piping above them. The changes implemented in 1812 were not all that sweeping. In full dress, admirals and captains now had white-faced lapels and lieutenants were allowed to wear the much-coveted epaulette. Admirals' epaulettes and embellishments remained unchanged, but captains' were given embellishments for the first time: a silver anchor for newly-promoted captains, and a silver anchor and crown for those with over three year's seniority. Commanders now wore a plain epaulette on each shoulder and a lieutenant one only, on his right shoulder.

One of the major changes concerned the cocked hat (also known as a "bicorn"), which had evolved from the early 18th century three-cornered tricorn. In the 1795 uniform this had a rear brim higher than that at the front, and was worn "athwartships" (i.e., with the points above the shoulders). Under the 1812 regulations, however, this changed to a hat with equal sized brims, which was worn "fore-and-aft" although admirals in full dress persisted (as was their prerogative) with the older, athwartships fashion well into the 1820s.

BELOW: The wardroom aboard HMS Gloucester (74), the stern windows provide good lighting and officers are waited upon by personal servants. The "walls" and "doors" on either side are painted canvas screens, which are stripped away whenever the ship goes to "action stations."

	Lapel	Cuff	Collar
ROYAL NAVY OFFICERS: UNDRESS UNIFORM DISTINCTIONS UNDER THE 1795-1812 REGULATIONS			
Admiral	Blue unlined with nine buttons	Three buttons – three stripes	Blue unlined
Vice-admiral		Three-buttons – two stripes	
Rear-admiral		Three buttons – one stripe	
Captain, Commander		Three buttons – no stripes	
Lieutenant, Sub-Lieutenant (from 1804)	Blue with white piping	Three buttons with one row of white piping.	Blue with white piping.
Midshipman	None	Three buttons	Blue with white collar patch.

RIGHT: An officer's cabin aboard HMS Gloucester, showing the spartan conditions in which even the officers lived. The "wall" on the left is a canvas screen separating this from the next cabin. The "window and curtains" are just paintings to give the occupant an illusion of homely living.

warrant officers coat with the Admiralty buttons.

Naval medical officers were also agitating for a proper uniform, and it should be borne in mind that the profession was divided into two divisions—physicians and surgeons. The former considered themselves superior, while the latter were further sub-divided into ship and hospital branches. Under the 1787 regulations, naval surgeons wore the same uniform as other warrant officers, but in 1805 they achieved a

LEFT: The physician's full dress was introduced in 1805. This would have been worn by Maturin on formal occasions.

BELOW: The master had wardroom status, good pay and one of the better cabins. The speaking trumpet was the symbol of his authority.

Warrant Officer

The 1787 dress regulations introduced uniforms for warrant officers and masters' mates, consisting of a civilian pattern, navy-blue coat, with lapels and turned back cuffs with three buttons, as worn by commissioned officers. They also wore a white waistcoat, breeches and stockings. Master's mates wore a very similar uniform, but without lapels and with white piping. Buttons were golden colour with an anchor, which was, in fact, the same design used by captains under the earlier regulations.

When new regulations were introduced in 1807 the cut of the coat was changed in certain minor respects, and new buttons introduced. For Masters and their mates these buttons bore the Navy Board crest, while for Pursers and their mates they carried the crest of the Victualling Office. The new regulations also introduced uniform for boatswains, carpenters and gunners, which was, in fact, the previous pattern

Fitting out.

ABOVE: Midshipman Blockhead "fitting out" for his first appointment. His weeping mother has bought every item on the clothing list and added many patent medicines to cure him of the ills she knows will befall him, while the unfortunate father checks the bill yet again to see if he can somehow reduce it! For the uncaring cause of all this, the reality of shipboard life will come as a terrible shock.

longed-for advance by being given the same status as Army surgeons and the uniform was altered to signify the new status. This took the form of a better quality coat with a stand-up collar, white waistcoat and breeches, while the buttons bore the crest of their parent body, the Sick and Hurt Board; ships surgeons had one button-hole on each side of the collar, while hospital surgeons had two. There were only a very few naval physicians and all were shore-based; they wore a similar uniform to the surgeons, but with a gold braid edging around the stand-up collar to indicate their superior status.

Midshipmen's dress was similar to, but much less grand than that of officers, and changed remarkably little over the period.

The uniform (there was no "full dress") consisted of a single-breasted blue coat with an upright collar carrying the badge of his position, a large white patch with a blue decorative hole and a small naval pattern button at the upper end. At the start of the period midshipmen wore a cocked hat, but they then became one of the first ranks to adopt the top hat.

Sailors

During 1792-1815, the position regarding uniform for petty officers and sailors was straightforward—there was none. When they joined, sailors initially continued to wear the clothes they already possessed, but

blue jacket over a white shirt, and white duck trousers, although HMS *Niger*'s boat crew dressed all in black; sailors rarely wore any form of footgear.

Royal Marines

For Royal Marines, a high standard of dress, uniformity and turnout were part of their way of life. Until 1802 Marines' officers wore long scarlet jackets with white facings and stand-up collar, silver epaulettes and a cocked hat worn "athwartships." Then in 1802 the high reputation of the corps and its steadiness during the mutinies of the late 1790s resulted in the award of the title "Royal" which, in turn, entitled the Corps to various embellishments to its uniforms. Thus the jacket facings were changed from white to

LEFT: Midshipman, undress, as worn from 1795. Note the top hat, large white gorget patch signifying his rank, and the dirk, a lighter sword than that used by officers.

these were gradually replaced from the Purser's "slops" and if there was a degree of similarity in dress it was usually achieved through the latter's bulk purchasing powers, rather than by deliberate intent. Some captains tried to exercise a degree of uniformity among their crew, and a few managed to ensure that their entire crew wore identical outfits. Most sailors were, of necessity, adept with needle and thread, and while all would have done repairs, some purchased material and made their own clothes. Some captains made their crews wear a standard form of headgear and the practice of carrying the ship's name on the sailor's hat appeared during the Napoleonic wars, being either painted on or embroidered on a ribbon.

Whatever sailors wore aboard ship, captains insisted that their boat's crew looked smart, for which a degree of uniformity was essential. This generally took the form of a standard headgear of some sort, a short

LEFT: There was no such thing as standard dress for sailors, although a degree of uniformity was achieved by the purser buying job lots of clothing for sale as "slops" to his crew.

RIGHT: Boatswain's mate
aboard HMS Gloucester
carries a rope "starter"
with which to
"encourage" lazy seamen;
in practice most just hit
whoever happened to be
nearest.

board was entirely covered in gold lace and fringed with gold.

Unlike the unfortunate sailors, Marine non-commissioned officers and privates not only had a standard uniform but were issued with a new one every year by the Navy Board. As with the officers this uniform was based on that of the army and when the royal title was conferred in 1802 the Marines' uniform was based on that of the First Footguards. Until 1807 corporals' rank was indicated by a shoulder knot, while sergeants wore both a knot and lace trimmings on their jackets. In 1807 this was brought into line with the Army—three large white chevrons for a sergeant, two for a corporal.

When at sea, Marines wore their full uniform for guard duties, parades, formal occasions and battle, but they also had a "working dress" which, like the sailors, usually consisted of items purchased from the Purser's slop room. Marines provided a number of men for gun crews aboard ship and in the (quite literal) heat of battle, may well have discarded their scarlet jackets.

blue, and metallic items such as epaulettes, buttons and lace changed from silver to gold.

As with naval and army officers, the style of the cocked hat changed from "athwartships" to "fore-and-aft." Royal Marine officers also wore a cockade in their hats, various colors indicating the detachment's base port: Chatham, Plymouth, or Portsmouth. All officers wore a red sash, an old-fashioned metal gorget, which hung around the neck, and a white sword belt slung over the right shoulder. All officers also wore epaulettes which were used to indicate rank —one on each shoulder for captains and just one (on the right shoulder) for lieutenants. Until 1802 these epaulettes were on a scarlet cloth base with looped braid and silver fringe, but these were changed to gold in 1802.

The design for these junior officers was changed again in 1810 when the shoulder

RIGHT: A ship's cook in
1799. Such appointments
were often a means of
giving continuing service
to seamen disabled in
battle. Culinary skills, if
any, were learnt on the
job.

LEFT: Artist's impression of how sailors enjoyed themselves in port. The men were not allowed ashore, so the women came aboard, and the officers looked the other way!

General Impression

Thus, the general impression aboard a man-of-war was of uniformity in some respects, but not in others. The naval commissioned and warrant officers were dressed in their respective uniforms and all Royal Marines were in their scarlet jackets unless employed on routine duties, while the petty officers and sailors, however, were dressed in a variety of clothing. There also appears to have been some form of hard weather clothing—an oil-skin jacket and hat—which was probably passed from one watch to another.

FAR LEFT: An officer of the Marines in full dress in 1796. The facings are white, while buttons, gorget plate and lacing are all of silver. The silver-edged hat with cockade is worn in the old "athwartships" style.

LEFT: After becoming the "Royal Marines," dress changed to blue facings, with gold lacing, buttons and gorget plate. The hat is now of the "fore-and-aft" pattern, with cockade indicating the division.

CHAPTER VI

OTHER NAVAL POWERS

The Royal Navy was opposed by numerous enemies during the years 1793 to 1815, of which by far the most important was the traditional enemy—France—although the United States Navy also proved itself a troublesome foe in the War of 1812. There were two major complicating factors for officers at sea. First, nations ashore changed sides and yesterday's enemy suddenly became today's ally and vice-versa. Secondly, news traveled very slowly and sometimes the first that a British captain knew of the outbreak of war was when a ship he had thought to be friendly suddenly opened fire. To give just one example, the USA declared war on Great Britain on June 19, 1812 and the first

the British admiral commanding at Rio de Janeiro knew of it was when a US merchant ship arrived on September 20—a full three months later!

France

England joined the War of the First Coalition in February 1793 and the Royal Navy immediately started offensive operations against the "old enemy." The English strategy throughout the following 24 years was to dominate the world's oceans, but the French never attempted such a role, their naval strategy being the maintenance of a "fleet in being" which concentrated only for specific operations, such as the invasion

RIGHT: The French Commerce de Marseille (120) was captured in 1793, but was found to be too weakly built for her enormous size and difficult to maneuver in shallow waters. She was converted into a troopship, but sailed so badly in a storm that she was taken back to England and converted into a prison ship. Expensive to maintain, she was broken up in 1802.

of Egypt, England or Ireland. A consequence of such a strategy was that the British blockades tended to keep French ships in harbor, with adverse effects on the latter's efficiency, training (both individual and collective), and morale. Nevertheless, the British always treated the French Navy with respect and knew that every engagement would be hard.

French naval architects had a well-deserved reputation for excellent designs and ships captured from the French tended to be highly regarded by their English crews. In fact, while the English often copied French design ideas, the French never felt the necessity to do the reverse. The French also tended to stick to standard designs; their line-of-battle ships being of just three designs, carrying 74, 80 and 120 guns, respectively. In the early years of the war the standard frigate mounted 36 guns, while the later, larger design mounted 44. The French also built many corvettes, which were direct equivalents of the English sloops, and operated many smaller, inshore vessels such as gunboats and tartans, particularly in the Mediterranean.

The French also employed large numbers

ABOVE: French naval architects had a reputation for excellence and the Royal Navy was usually very happy to take a captured French warship into service, such as this French frigate, seen here in about 1780, which would then have served well into the Napoleonic period.

BELOW: Engagements between American and British ships were always hard fought, as in this fight between USS Constitution (44) and HMS Java (38) on December 29, 1812. Seen here, Java, crippled but still fighting, approaches Constitution to board her, but first her foremast goes by the board and then the maintopmast is shot away, crippling her. With defeat absolutely certain, the British ship had no choice but to strike.

of privateers, because the English merchant fleet was a very attractive target for the *guerre de corse*. The other factor, however, was that the English blockade confined French fishing fleets to harbor, putting many fishermen out of work, who then provided eager recruits for privateers.

Spain

Spain had three centuries of experience with overseas operation, spreading and then defending its huge empire. In the Americas this included Florida, Louisiana and across to the Pacific shore, virtually all of Central America, and most of southern America except for what now constitutes Argentina, Brazil and Chile. Its other terri-

tories were in the Far East, and included the Carolines, Marianas and Philippines. It thus required a large navy and one of its warships was the largest in the world, the *Santissima Trinidad*, a four-decker armed with 130 guns, which was completed in 1769 in Havana. The main type, however, as with all major navies, was the 74, and these Spanish ships were always treated with respect by the Royal Navy. The Spanish also operated a number of galleys and xebecs in the Mediterranean.

The Spanish economic system depended heavily on the regular arrival of treasure ships from its overseas possessions, and these were always a dream target for the Royal Navy because of the enormous prize money involved. Like other countries, Spain

changed sides several times during the period and at the time of Trafalgar (October 21, 1805) Spanish ships formed part of a combined fleet with the French. From 1808 onwards, however, the French started to take over Spanish naval bases and the Spanish fleet virtually ceased to exist.

United States

Following the War of Independence, the small US Navy was disbanded, but had to be recreated in 1794, primarily in order to combat the depredations of Barbary pirates operating out of Algiers and several new frigates were laid down, although this particular problem was resolved before they were completed. Naval problems contin-

ued, first with France in the "Quasi-War" of 1798-1800, and then with another lot of Barbary pirates, this time based in Tripoli. Meanwhile, the habit of many RN captains of stopping US merchant ships and impressing any sailors who were either of proven British nationality or even suspected of it caused increasing friction. There were several actual fights, including those between USS *Chesapeake* and HMS *Leopard* in 1807 and USS *President* versus HMS *Little Belt* in 1811, and the two countries then drifted into a state of open war in 1812.

The main strength of the US fleet in the naval operations of 1812-14 lay in its large frigates, which were well-built and well-armed and always fought hard. The largest of them, the 44s, were roughly the size of a

ABOVE: American topsail schooner, Catherine, armed with 14 six-pounders, flies the British flag as a ruse de guerre whilst approaching a possible prize. Discovering that it is the British sloop-of-war HMS Pylades (16), her captain sensibly puts down the helm to flee. As he does so, he flies the taunting message "Catch Me Who Can". On this occasion nobody did, but on July 26, 1812 he was caught by HMS Colibri (16).

British 74, but with a lighter armament. In essence, they were similar to the battlecruisers of a century later, being able to outfight anything they could catch and to outsail anything that outgunned them. On the outbreak of war the US Navy's operational fleet comprised three 44-gun frigates (Constitution, President and United States), three smaller frigates (John Adams, Congress and Essex), five sloops and two brigs. There were five more frigates in reserve (three of which were returned to operational status) and some 150-plus gunboats of which 62 were actually in service.

The naval war was in three phases, each approximating to a calendar year. Thus the first phase, in 1812, saw a series of US strategic initiatives, with a US squadron and individual frigates patrolling in the Atlantic, and major successes in single-ship

engagements. In 1813 the British imposed a coastal blockade, which was intended to stop all commercial traffic and also to keep the frigates in harbor. Despite this, a number of US ships did get to sea, notably USS *Essex*, which sailed down the Atlantic and around Cape Horn, wreaking havoc among British merchantmen and whalers as she went. In 1814 Napoleon abdicated thus freeing the Royal Navy to turn its full attention on the war with the USA, but the war ended with the Treaty of Ghent.

Netherlands

The United Provinces covered what is now the Netherlands and Belgium, and while they had had a powerful navy some decades earlier, by 1792 the numbers of both ships and men had decreased, although both con-

BELOW: The privateers enabled America to take the war against Britain to European waters. Here the schooner David Porter *rides out a storm in the Bay of Biscay on January 30, 1814, her only sail a well-reefed spanker. Not visible is the sea-anchor, fashioned from a spare yard, that kept her head to wind.*

tinued to be of good quality. The United Provinces were very vulnerable to land attack and spent most of the wars occupied by the French, the two countries were finally amalgamated in 1810. The problem for the Royal Navy was that an enemy fleet, whether Dutch or combined Dutch/French, in the Scheldt area was a major threat to southern England, and it spent many years blockading the major exits past Flushing in the south and the Texel Channel further north.

Denmark

At the time of the Napoleonic Wars, the kingdoms of Denmark and Norway were joined. With few colonies to protect, the navy was small its main strategic role being to defend Danish coastal waters. The Danish fleet was depleted in the two Battles of Copenhagen (1801 and 1807), after which they concentrated on small gunboats.

Sweden

Sweden had one or two major warships, including *Gustav IV Adolph*, 76, but concentrated mainly on gunboats to harass enemy ships in the offshore archipelagoes. Like other Baltic navies, the Swedes also operated some galleys and oared-gunboats.

ABOVE: A Russian vessel, equivalent to a British ship-rigged sloop towing a felucca, also flying the Russian flag. The Russian Navy changed sides several times, but served alongside the Royal Navy in 1795-99 and 1812-15, and even the hardened British sailors thought that their Russian equivalents were poorly fed and harshly treated!

Russia

The Russian Navy suffered from the geographical problem that has plagued it down to the present day in that it had to serve in the Arctic Ocean and the Baltic and Black Seas, none of which had guaranteed access to the open ocean, nor were they mutually supporting. (There were also naval units in the Caspian Sea and on the Siberian rivers, but these were not relevant to the wars in Europe.) Thus, the exit from the Black Sea was controlled by Turkey, while the Baltic exit was controlled by Denmark and Sweden; further, the Baltic and the Arctic Ocean were icebound for many months of the year.

Russia changed sides several times,

RIGHT: A typical Mediterranean galley; this particular example belongs to the Kingdom of Naples and is lying at anchor off Castel Vecchio in Leghorn. The long spiron (prow) was not a vestigial ram, but was needed as a belaying point for the tack of the forward lateen.

which had obvious implications for the naval war. Russia sided with Britain and her allies from 1795 to 1799, but then made peace with the French. The Russians re-entered the war on the allied side in 1805 but made peace with Napoleon at Tilsit in 1807 and then cooperated with the French until 1812. At that point Napoleon invaded Russia, and the tsar once again joined the anti-French coalition. The Imperial Russian Navy designed and constructed its own ships, usually with foreign assistance, and maintained a sizeable fleet, although its strength was dissipated by its geographical splits. The ships were not particularly well built but were of some assistance to the Royal Navy, serving against the French in the North Sea and Mediterranean in 1795-99, and again in 1812-15. Conditions aboard Russian ships reflected the social divisions in Russia and even Royal Navy sailors, whose lives were by no means comfortable, considered the Russian sailors to be harshly treated.

Ottoman Empire

The Ottoman Empire was a huge, sprawling and poorly controlled collection of territories, under the nominal rule of Turkey. This included the north African littoral from what is now Algeria, through Tunisia and Tripoli (now Libya) to Egypt, then northwards along the coast of what was then known as the Levant to Syria and Turkey itself. In what was nominally Europe it controlled Greece, Albania and what was until recently Yugoslavia. At the turn of the 18th/19th century it had a large fleet, whose primary purpose was to provide control in its empire and to challenge Russia in the Black Sea. The Russia Navy, as always, was frustrated by the fact that Turkey controlled the very narrow Bosporus, which gave the only exit to the Mediterranean, and could exercise tight control over its use.

CHAPTER VII

PRIVATEERS & PIRATES

Lurking on the fringes of the naval war were privateers who obeyed few rules and pirates who obeyed none. The British economy depended upon seagoing trade, ranging from coasters around the seaboard of the British Isles, through the large Baltic, Mediterranean and Caribbean trade, to the global routes to South America and the Far East. All of this involved thousands of merchant vessels which provided ample opportunity for the type of warfare known as *guerre de course*.

Letters of Marque

Commercial seagoing captains could obtain governmental authority known as the letter of marque and reprisal (usually shortened to Letter Of Marque). This ancient legal device was originally intended to enable a private citizen to obtain redress for a wrong committed by a foreign national after other forms of legal action had failed. Over the centuries, this particular aspect fell into abeyance, but the legal concept was used to authorize a private citizen to "distress and destroy" his country's enemies in times of war.

By the 1790s, Letters of Marque were issued to named individuals for a specific vessel and against a defined enemy, and was a considerable mutual convenience to all concerned except, of course, the enemy. The government obtained the services of a warship and crew at no cost to itself, while the privateer obtained authority to conduct warlike operations, take prizes, and generally act as a legalized pirate, and, if successful, to make very considerable profits. The US privateer, *America*, for example, earned her owners $600,000 during the War of 1812, a very considerable sum by the standards of the day.

A pretext of "legal process" was maintained by ordering that prizes be handled using the same system as for naval prizes, which, in the British case, meant through the High Court of Admiralty in London or the authorized Prize Courts in most colonies. Once the prize money was awarded, however, the privateer's owners and crew received the whole lot and shared it out among themselves according to their own arrangements, which was normally in accordance with a written contract. Other countries had similar arrangements according to their own laws and the example opposite shows the form used by the United States in the "Quasi-War".

The system was not without its drawbacks. Nations found the enemy's privateers a considerable nuisance and it was by no means unknown for captured crewmen to be hanged as pirates, even when they were able to provide valid letters of marque. Also, since the privateers were freelancers, they were under no form of either strategic or tactical control by the naval chain-of-command. Flags were often a matter of convenience and while many privateers stuck to the rules (such as they were) by flying their own national flag and attacking only their country's legal enemies, others were not so careful. Thus, in 1793-4 the French ambassador in the United States issued Letters of Marque to US-owned and

JOHN ADAMS, PRESIDENT of the UNITED STATES of AMERICA

To all who shall see these Presents, Greeting:

Know Ye, THAT in pursuance of an Act of Congress of the United States in this case provided, passed on the ninth day of July, one thousand seven hundred and ninety-eight, I have commissioned, and by these presents do commission the private armed Ship called the Herald of the burthen of *Threehundredtwentyfive* tons, or thereabouts, owned by *Ebenezer Preble & Samuel Parkman of Boston Merchants, & Nathaniel Silsbee of Salem Mariner, all in the State of Massachusetts mounting Ten* Carriage guns, and navigated by Thirty men; hereby licensing and authorizing *Nathaniel Silsbee* captain, and *Nathaniel Hathorne 1st & Alexander Anderson 2nd* lieutenants of the said *Ship* and the other officers and crew thereof to subdue, seize and take any armed French vessel which shall be found within the jurisdictional limits of the United States or elsewhere on the high seas; and such captured vessel, with her apparel, guns and appurtenances, and the goods or effects which shall be found on board the same, together with all French persons and others, who shall be found acting on board, to bring within some port of the United States, which may have been captured by any French armed vessel; in order that proceedings may be had concerning such capture or re-capture in due form of law, and as to right and justice shall prevail. This commission to continue in force during the pleasure of the President of the United States for the time being. Given under my Hand and the Seal of the United States of America, at Philadelphia, the *twentysecond* day of *January* in the year of our Lord, one thousand *eight* hundred and of the Independence of the said States, the twenty*fourth*.

[Signed: John Adams, President]
[Signed: Timothy Pickering, Secretary of State]

ABOVE: Transcript of Letter of Marque issued by President Adams, July 9, 1798.

ABOVE: All privateers
needed was a 'Letter of
Marque' from their
government to enable
them to start attacking the
enemy on a commercial
basis. Here, the French
privateer Unité attacks the
British commercial cutter
Swan in 1797, Once
successful, the prize will
be sent into the nearest
friendly port, where first
the cargo and then the
ship will be sold.

for an attack, without the benefit of a Letter of Marque. A particular group of such people were the so-called picaroons, who were based on French territories such as Guadeloupe, and attacked British merchantmen in the Caribbean.

In France this type of warfare was known as *guerre de course*, which resulted in their English name of corsairs. Many were based on ports on the Channel, but they also operated in the Atlantic, Mediterranean and the Caribbean.

During the years that she was neutral in the war between England and France, the United States developed a series of fast commercial vessels, designed to transport low-volume/high-value cargoes between Europe and the United States. When war with Britain broke out in 1812, these proved ideal privateers, still serving as cargo-carriers but with letters of marque which enabled them to attack targets of opportunity. Well over 500 US-registered vessels were issued with letters of marque during the war.

These vessels carried an armament sufficient to overcome all but the best armed

—manned vessels, which then sailed under the French flag to operate against English vessels. In another variation, vessels carried numbers of national flags and documents, assuming a new nationality according to the needs of the moment.

Some privateers were as large and powerful as frigates, and in addition to attacking merchant vessels were not averse to taking on smaller warships, such as brigs, if the situation seemed favorable. Other craft were simple rowing-boats, although most of these were little more than pirates, local fishermen who seized a passing opportunity

RIGHT: Cutaway drawing
of a Mediterranean galley.
The major areas below
decks are: A. sick quarters;
B. secure vault; C. sail
stores; D, F, G. holds; E.
magazine; H, I, K. living
quarters. Note the lateen
sails, short tiller arm
(which must have made
maneuvering difficult)
and the long prow.

merchantmen, but were little match for a man-of-war, from which the privateer would normally flee making use of its excellent speed – and, in the case of those carrying a fore-and-aft rig, making good use of their abilities to "point" much better to windward. One particularly cheeky US privateer actually had a flag bearing the message "Catch me who can" which she flew to aggravate English captains vainly pursuing her (but her luck ran out on July 26, 1812 when she was caught and captured by HM Sloop Colibri). Privateers also carried large crews, both to take the targets by boarding and to form prize crews to take them back to port.

One advantage of privateering for both France and the USA was that they could take the naval war to the very shores of the British Isles and many coasters were captured. Not surprisingly, this caused great embarrassment to both the government and the Royal Navy, compelling the latter to deploy large numbers of warships on convoy duties, involving ships and manpower which could not then, of course, be deployed in more distant waters on more offensive tasks.

Privateers were by no means always successful. The American ship, *Comet*, for example, was a very successful privateer with a good captain and crew, but when they attacked the British transport *Hibernia* on January 10, 1814 the battle lasted for some 10 hours and *Comet* eventually had to withdraw.

A particular hazard for British ships was when more than one small privateer cooperated with each other, particularly when several rowing boats joined in an attack on a becalmed warship. Even then the enemy was not always successful. For example, HM *Cutter Entrepenante* (8) was lying becalmed near Faro castle near Malaga in 1811 when she was attacked by four lateen-rigged privateers which were also equipped with sweeps, but in a hard-fought action lasting many hours *Entrepenante* fought off her attackers.

Piracy

Even though Letters of Marque were so easy to obtain, pirates still plied their ancient trade, with Greek pirates in the

BELOW: Pirates in feluccas attacking the Honorable East India Company's (HEIC) ship, Aurora. She is wearing the flag of the HEIC, consisting of a Union flag (pre-1801) in the canton with 13 horizontal red and white stripes.

ABOVE: Pirates were notoriously merciless. These Javanese pirates have attacked the British brig, Admiral Trowbridge, and her master, although seriously wounded, has been secured to the capstan and put in leg irons, which are being nailed to the deck.

Aegean, Arabs in the Gulf, Bugis, Chinese and Malays in the South China Sea, and almost every known nationality in the Caribbean. One of the more dramatic confrontations between the Royal Navy and pirates was an engagement which took place off the Spanish coast in August 1798. The British vessel was HMS *L'Espoir*, a 14-gun sloop with a crew of 70, commanded by Commander Loftus Otway. *L'Espoir* was escorting a convoy when she espied a large vessel approaching with the clear intention of attacking and it was immediately clear that she was much larger and more powerful. In fact, it was only after the battle that it was established that she was the *Liguria*, a former Dutch frigate, armed with 12 18-pounders, four 12-pounders, ten 6-pounders and a number of smaller pieces, and manned by a crew of 120. This

powerful vessel was operating out of Genoa, captained by a Spaniard, with a crew of all nationalities and with no claim to a letter of marque; in other words, a pirate. Despite the obvious disparity of force, Otway immediately headed for the enemy. The battle lasted four hours and ended with the pirate's defeat and it caused a sensation three days later in Gibraltar when *L'Espoir* entered the port, flying a modest signal asking for assistance in towing her prize, which was twice her size, had twice her crew, and twice the armament.

Barbary States

"Barbary pirates" were a particular menace, benefiting from the fact that the European countries were too busy fighting each other to do anything to restrain them.

The term "barbary" stemmed from an Arab buccaneer named Khair ad-Din and nicknamed Barbarossa (red beard) whose reputation led to the whole of the north African coastline being labeled the "barbarine (or barbary) states".

Tripoli, Tunisia, and Algeria were nominally part of the Ottoman Empire but in reality virtually autonomous, while the kingdom of Morocco was fully independent. All four provided bases for pirates who inflicted a reign of terror on commercial trade in the Mediterranean and eastern Atlantic, their rulers, known as *deys*, imposed a system of taxation under which those operating out of his port paid him a fixed percentage of all income from looting, ransom money and sale of slaves. It was a form of privateering, except that there was no formal state of war involved; in reality it was state-sponsored piracy.

By the 1790s the power of the Barbary states had diminished, but their fearsome reputation remained and most European maritime nations continued to pay "fees" for the safe passage of their shipping through north African waters—the modern term is "protection racket."

Following the War of Independence, US vessels were no longer protected by the Royal Navy, and Barbary pirates started to seize American ships and put their crews into slavery. In 1799, in an effort to overcome this, the US government agreed to make regular payments to all four rulers, but in 1801 the Pasha of Tripoli raised his demands, and when the US government refused to pay, he declared war. The US sent naval squadrons to the Mediterranean and for some time there was desultory action. In 1804 however, Lieutenant Stephen Decatur led an attack on Tripoli harbor which Lord Nelson described as "the most daring act of the age" There was another major assault in 1805." by the US Marines on Derna and peace was achieved in 1806.

BELOW: Greek pirates in the Adriatic. Such freebooters were a common threat to commercial trading vessels.

GLOSSARY OF NAUTICAL TERMS

Aback. When a sail's forward surface is pressed upon by the wind.

Abaft. Hinder part of a ship, some point nearer the stern.

Abeam. An area roughly at right angles to the ship's mainmast.

Aboard. The inside of a ship; thus, a person entering a ship *goes aboard. Fall aboard* meant that one ship collided with another.

Adrift: A ship broken loose from its moorings.

Aft, After. Towards the stern.

Amidships. Central part of a ship.

Armed en flute. See **flute.**

Astern. Behind the vessel.

Athwart. Across, as in "athwartship."

Athwart the forefoot. Firing a round across another ship's bows.

Aweigh. Anchor hanging vertically, clear of the seabed; hence "anchor's aweigh" meant "ready to proceed."

Avast. "Stop hauling on a rope," or, generally, stop doing something.

Bar. Shoal formed by the tides at the mouth of a river or harbor.

Bare poles. Having no sails up.

Barricade. See "Bulwark."

Barge. 1. Cargo carrier used on rivers canals and coastal waters. 2. naval boat for senior officers (e.g., captains and admirals).

Batten Down. To close and secure all the openings in the weather decks.

Beam. 1. Greatest breadth of ship. 2. Strong baulk of timber.

Beam Ends. Ship in extreme distress, lying on her side was "on her beam ends."

Bear up/away. To alter the course from close-hauled to running before the wind.

Bearing. Situation of any object in reference to a part of the ship.

Beat to quarters. Crew called to action stations by drum.

Beating. Making progress against the wind in a zigzag line.

Becalmed. Ship motionless due to a lack of wind.

Becket. Short length of rope with an eye at one end and a double-walled knot at the other.

Bed. Wooden base on which a gun or mortar was mounted.

Belay. Make fast; stop doing something.

Bend/bent. To knot one rope to another; or to secure the sails to the yards.

Between Decks ('tweendecks.) Space between upper and lowest decks in a ship.

Bight. Any part of a rope between the ends; collar formed by a rope.

Bilge. Flat part of the ship's internal bottom. "To be bilged" was to be holed on the bottom of the ship, e.g., by a rock.

Binnacle. Cabinet mounted immediately before the wheel.

Birth (or berth). Place of anchorage for a ship; or an individual's cabin.

Bitt. Device for belaying cables, ropes, etc.

Bitter end. Inboard end of a ship's cable, which was belayed to a "bitt;" thus, "to the bitter end" means to reach the end of something.

Boarding. Enter an enemy ship by force.

Bobstay. Stay from the nose of the bowsprit to the stem near the waterline.

Bomb vessel. Vessel carrying a heavy mortar:

Boom. 1. Light spar extending a yard to carry an additional sail; e.g., studding-sail boom. 2. Floating defense consisting of baulks of timber linked by lengths of rope/chain.

Bow. Forward part of the vessel.

Bower anchor. Main working anchor, carried at the bow.

Bowlines. Ropes made fast to the leeches (sides) of the sail to pull them forward.

Bowsprit. Mast protruding from the bow to support the foremast stays.

LEFT: A xebec lies at anchor off the lighthouse at Naples. The mixed lateen and square rig was developed by corsairs for speed and maneuverability. Also, unlike a galley, it had a heavy broadside battery.

Breeching (breech rope). Stout rope restraining a gun's recoil.

Brig. Vessel with two masts, both square-rigged, but with a fore-and-aft, gaff-rigged driver.

Brigantine. Two-masted vessel, square-rigged to topgallants on the foremast, but fore-and-aft rigged on the main with a topmast.

Bring-to. To arrange sails to counteract each other, keeping a ship stationary.

Broach-to. Vessel inadvertently slews round, until broadside to the waves and in danger of losing its masts.

Broadside. Firing all guns on one side of the ship.

Bulkhead. Any internal vertical wall not formed by the ship's side.

Bulwark. The side of ship from the deck to the gunwale (also called **barricade**).

Burgoo. Type of meat stew.

Burthen. Measure of a vessel's carrying capacity in tons.

By the board. Over the side.

Cable. 1. Nautical measure; one cable equals 1/10th nautical mile. 2. Anchor rope or chain.

Caliber. Diameter of the bore of a gun.

Capstan. Vertical, deck-mounted barrel for lifting heavy weights.

Captain. 1. Naval rank. 2. Commanding officer of any vessel. 3. Able seaman with specific responsibility; e.g., captain of the top, captain of the gun.

Carronade. Short barreled weapon made by Carron Ironworks.

Carvel-built. Planks laid side by side, the gap being filled by pitch.

Cat, cat-o'nine-tails. Instrument of punishment made from nine lengths of cord, with three knots at the end of each and spliced to a short length of thick rope to form a handle.

Catharpins. Short ropes seized to the upper part of the lower shrouds.

Caulk. Filling gaps between planks with oakum, which was then sealed with molten pitch.

Chains. Metal fittings on side of the hull to which shrouds were attached.

Chase. 1. Outward portion of gun between trunnion and muzzle. 2. Gun firing forward or astern (as opposed to the broadside).

Chasse-marée. French coastal craft, usually a lugger.

Chronometer. Maritime timepiece used to work out longitude.

Clew. 1. Lower corners of square sails and the after corner of a fore-and-aft sail. 2. Clew-line (clew garnet on courses), a tackle to hoist the sail to the yard.

Clinker-built. Construction with one plank overlapping another.

Close-hauled. To sail as close to the wind as possible.

Corvette. Small French warship, equivalent to English sloop.

Course. Lowest sail on a particular mast.

Crank. Ship unable to carry too much sail with safety.

Crossjack yard. Yard to which the mizen topsail was brought down.

Cross-tree. Strut at right-angles to the mast, spreading the shrouds.

Cutter. 1. Single-masted, gaff-rigged coastal vessel with more than one head-sail. 2. Warship's boat.

Cutwater. Timber at the front of the stem; technically, the knee of the head.

D.D. Abbreviation for "discharged dead."

Davit. Piece of timber used as a crane to hoist the flukes of the anchor to the top of the bow, a process known as "fishing the anchor."

Deck-head. Underside of the deck above.

Dolphin-Striker. Small spar at right-angles to and below the bowsprit.

Draught. 1. Drawing of ship's lines. 2. Distance between waterline and bottom of keel, when fully loaded.

Driver. Another name for spanker.

Ease, seats of. Contemporary euphemism for toilets. (See also Heads.)

Fathom. Nautical unit for depth or length. 1 fathom = 6 feet.

Flaked. Cable either stowed or laid out ready for use.

Fleet. Assemblage of more than 10 warships.

Flotilla. Assemblage of smaller warships.

Fluke. Broad part (palms) of an anchor.

Flush decked. Vessel without quarterdeck or forecastle.

Flute, armed en flute. Vessel carrying less than its usual establishment of guns.

Freeboard. Distance between the waterline and the lowest port sill.

Foot. Bottom edge of sail.

Fore-and-aft. See 'sails'.

Forecastle. Extra deck forward for handling jibs.

Forestay (headstay). Stay running from the head of the foremast to the stem.

Forward. Front end of the vessel.

Founder. To sink in open water (i.e., not due to striking a rock or running aground).

Frame. Structural ribs forming the hull.

ABOVE: A midshipman's berth in a British frigate at sea.

Furl. To wrap or roll a sail close to the yard, stay or mast.

Futtock shrouds. Short lengths of rope fitted immediately below the tops. Shortened form of "foot-hook."

Gaff. Short spar mounted above a fore-and-aft sail.

Galleon. 16th century term for large ship; retained by Royal Navy to describe any Spanish vessel carrying a valuable cargo.

Gig. Small ship's boat.

Grapple. To attach one ship to another in battle.

Gudgeon. Metal bracket with ring.

Gunboat. Small boat armed with one or two heavy guns.

Gun-deck. Deck(s) on which the main (heaviest) battery was placed.

Gun salute. Succession of shots fired in honor of important personages.

Gunshot. "Within gunshot" meant range of long cannon; i.e., about 1-1$\frac{1}{4}$ miles.

Gunwale. The timbers along the tops of the bulwarks.

Halyard (haul-yard). Rope used to raise/lower a yard.

Hand. 1. To furl and lower a sail. 2. A sailor or member of the crew.

Hawse hole. Opening in the bow for the anchor cable.

Hawser. A small cable.

Heads. Small platforms either side of the stem, which were used as latrines by the crew. Also known as Seats of Ease.

Headsail. Triangular fore-and-aft sail.

Heave-to. Reduce to minimum sails in heavy weather.

Heave down. Lower topmasts, etc.

Hogging. Stress on a ship's hull when the bows and stern dip relative to the more buoyant amidships section; if too great will result in catastrophe.

Hulk. Old ship stripped of masts and guns, used for accommodation, receiving recruits, holding prisoners-of-war or as hospitals.

Idler. Member of ship's crew not on the watch-keeping roster.

Jury Rig. Makeshift device to replace something damaged until more permanent repairs can be made; e.g., to enable a dismasted vessel reach the nearest port.

Ketch. Rig with no foremast and a mainmast placed well aft, taller than the mizenmast.

Knee. Right-angled baulk of timber joining a deck beam to the side frame of a ship.

Knot. Nautical measurement of speed; 1 knot equals 1 nautical mile per hour (1.153 statute miles per hour).

Labor. A ship pitching and rolling heavily in rough seas.

Lanyard. Short length of rope used to make something secure or to serve as a handle.

Larboard. Left-hand side of the vessel, looking forward.

Large. A large wind was one crossing the line of a ship's course on the beam or quarter.

Lateen. Fore-and-aft rig with large triangular sail bent to long yard hoisted to a relatively short mast.

Latitude. Position on the Earth's surface, measured as an angle from the Equator; e.g., 40° 45' North. 1 degree of latitude = 60 nautical miles.

Launch. Type of ship's boat.

League. 1 league = 3 nautical miles = 1/20th degree.

Lee. Side of a vessel opposite to that from which the wind is blowing. Thus, a "ship to leeward" was one downwind, while a "lee-shore" meant the wind was pushing the ship down towards the land.

Lift. Rope from the masthead to the yardarm used to adjust the angle of the yard.

Loblolly. Thick oatmeal gruel, considered to have medicinal properties.

Loblolly Boy. Surgeon's assistant, who, among other duties, gave the soup to the patients.

Lobscouse. Sailor's dish made of stewed meat, vegetables and ship's biscuit (as were virtually all sailors' meals!); usually shortened to *scouse*.

Longitude. Position of a point on the Earth's surface measured as an angle east or west of the Greenwich meridian (0°); e.g., 32° 21' East

Loose-footed. Sail secured to a boom only at its forward point (tack) and after end (clew).

Lugger. Boat with large, quadrilateral, fore-and-aft sail bent to a sprit, attached to the mast at a point about one-third of its length; a common rig in northern, Channel and Mediterranean waters.

Masts. The highest mast was always the **Main Mast** and carried the principal sails; the forward mast was the **foremast**, the after mast the **mizen mast**.

Messenger. Small rope, formed as an endless loop lashed to the anchor cable to lead it around the capstan.

Miss stays. A vessel "missed stays"

when she failed to go about from one tack to another.

Nautical Mile. 1 nautical mile = 6,080 feet = 1 minute of latitude.

Nipper. Stop or strop used temporarily to seize two ropes together, particularly the anchor cable and messenger.

Oakum. Teased-out fibres of unwanted hemp rope, used for **caulking** (q.v.) seams.

Ordinary. A ship "in ordinary" was out of commission, with a small complement, but including the "standing officers."

Ordnance, Board of. Independent Government department responsible for providing weapons, ammunition and some stores to the navy and army. The Board was headed by a distinguished soldier—Master-General of the Ordnance— but was not a part of the Army/War Office.

Orlop. Series of platforms in the hold in smaller ships; in larger ships a light deck.

Packet. Small, fast Post office vessel for carrying mail.

Partner. Hole in deck through which mast passed.

Pendant. 1. Long, narrow flag with split tail flown from the masthead of warships in commission. 2. Shorter, swallow-tailed burgee worn by the ship of the senior officer of a squadron (broad pendant). 3. Assembly of short ropes used in hoisting heavy items such as boats.

Pierced. Number of gunports.

Pinnace. Ship's boat used to transport junior officers around a harbor/ anchorage

Pitching. Longitudinal movement of ship in which bows go down and the stern rises, and vice-versa.

Plying. Turning to windward.

Polacre. Mediterranean vessel with two or three masts , usually with a very large lateen sail on the fore-mast, but square-rigged on the others.

Port. Left-hand side of the vessel, looking forward.

Portable soup. A soup concentrated into solid tablets and dispensed by the doctor for its supposed medicinal benefits.

Post-Captain. An officer of captain's rank commanding a seagoing 6th rate or larger.

Post-ship. 6th rates, with 20-24 guns, were known as a "post-ship" to differentiate it from a sloop.

Pound. Guns were rated by the weight of the solid shot they fired; e.g., 32-pounder. (See table on page 56).

Powder Monkey. Member of gun-crew responsible for carrying cartridges from the magazine to the gun.

Preventer. Rope, chain or fitting backing-up rigging, spars, cables, etc, or limiting their movement. Usually set up before battle or in anticipation of bad weather.

Quadrant. Navigational instrument for measuring angles.

Quarter. After end of either side of a vessel.

Quarterdeck. Deck running from the after end of the waist and above it to the stern.

Rake. 1. Firing at an enemy ship from either ahead or astern, so that the shot travelled along the length of the ship. 2. Angle of inclination of masts, bowsprit, stern or stern-post.

Ratlines. Ropes secured across

shrouds to form ladders.

Rates/Rating System. The Royal Navy classified its ships according to a rating system, depended on the number of guns carried—see page 11.

Raze/Razee. French term denoting a reconstructed warship in which a deck level was removed; e.g., converting a two-decker ship-of-the-line into a single-decker frigate.

Reef. To reduce the area of a sail by rolling or folding part of it in anticipation of, or during heavy weather.

Rigging. Ropes comprising the rig, which fell into two types. 1. Standing Rigging supported the masts and was tarred to extend its life. 2. Running Rigging was used to raise, lower and control the sails and to move spars; it was not tarred.

Rolling. Lateral movement of a ship.

Royals. Square sails above the top-gallants, used in light winds.

Sails. Sails were either square, i.e., approximately rectangular in shape and rigged across the hull, or fore-and-aft, i.e., four-sided or triangular, but rigged along the line of the hull. Sails, which were bent to yards/booms, spread when making sail, and handed when taking in.

Scud. Running before the wind.

Scupper. Metal-lined drainage holes in the ship's sides.

Scuttle. Sink a ship by cutting a hole in the bottom.

Send Down. To dismount and lower large spar, topmast or yard.

Shank. Main shaft of an anchor.

Sheathing. Protective layer of copper around ships' bottoms.

Sheers. Yards lashed together at one end and raised to provide a lifting tackle; e.g., for raising masts.

Sheer hulk. Hulk equipped with sheer legs, primarily used to raise the lower masts of ships moored alongside.

Sheet. Rope attached to the lower corner of sails to control the tautness of the sail.

Slings. Supports for the yards.

Shallop. Small sailing vessel.

Ship. 1. Sailing vessel with three masts; "ship-rigged." 2. To install something in its proper position.

Shrouds. Rope stays supporting the mast.

Sloop. Small warship, marginally smaller than a sixth-rate, but larger than a brig. Variations included: **ship-rigged sloop** with three masts; **brig-rigged sloop** with two; **quarterdeck sloops** with a quarterdeck and **flush-decked sloops** without.

Slops. Clothing and personal equipment issued on repayment by the Purser.

Snow. Two-masted vessel with a gaff-headed main course.

Sounding. Process ascertaining the depth of water.

Spanker. Fore-and-aft sail rigged abaft the mainmast, or mizen, if fitted.

Spar-deck. A deck over the waist, linking the forecastle and quarterdeck.

Splice. Unite broken strands of rope.

Spreader. Struts holding the shrouds away from the mast.

Spring. Mast, yard or other spar split by an overpress of sail, heavy pitch or jerk.

Sprit. A strong beam.

Squadron. An assemblage of less than 10 ships.

Square-rigged. Rig in which the principal sails are approximately rectangular in shape.

Standing Rigging. See rigging.

Starboard. Right-hand side of the vessel, looking forward.

Start. To move from rest, loosen or break out.

Starter. Short length of rope used by boatswains mates to hit sailors who appeared slow in performing a task.

Stay. 1. Rope supporting mast from forward. Fore-and-aft sails bent to such stays were known as "staysails." 2. To stay a ship was to

ABOVE: Ready Marines by the Right Dress. A sudden squal during drill.

arrange the sails and move the rudder so as to bring the ship's head into the wind in order to get her on the other tack—see also **miss stays**.

Stem. Timber beam forming the forward extremity of the hull.

Stern. Extreme after part of the hull.

Stiff. A vessel with a stable design, capable of carrying a reasonable amount of sail in all weathers; opposite of crank.

Storm Sail. Special sails made of the strongest canvas and of reduced area, for use in heavy weather.

Strike colors. To haul down the national flag as a sign of surrender.

Studding sail. Additional square sails set outboard of principal sails, with removable yards and booms.

Sweep. Long oar used in smaller vessels.

Tack. 1. Sailing with the wind, when it is coming from any direction but aft. 2. To change direction by putting the bow through the wind.

Taffrail. Top rail around the stern, between the two gunwales.

Tartane. Vessel with large lateen sail and jib, noted for exceptional speed, usually some 50-60 feet long.

Tender. Lacking in stability; i.e., the same as "crank" and the opposite of "stiff."

Thrum. To thread short pieces of yarn through a sail to increase its effectiveness when lowered overboard to stop a leak or hole.

Thwart. Boards placed across a boat, upon which people sat.

Topgallant. Above the topmast and below the royals; hence, topgallant mast, topgallant sails, etc.

Tonnage. Notional figure, based on the approximation that 100 cubic feet of internal volume was equivalent to 1 ton in weight. The Royal Navy used the formula **Tonnage = Length x breadth x _ breadth ÷ 94,** where the length was from the *outside* of the stem to the *outside* of the sternpost, and the breadth was measured *over* the planking, all being in feet. The US Navy used a marginally different system, where the divisor was 95, the length was measured from the *inside* of the posts and the breadth was measured across the frames and *excluded* the planking.

Top. Platform at the lower masthead, primarily intended to spread the topmast shrouds, but also serving as a place for lookouts and sharpshooters in battle.

Top hamper. All masts, rigging, spars, booms, etc.

Traveller. Hoop moving along a mast or spar.

Truck. Small wooden disk used as a wheel; e.g. on the gun carriage.

Trunnions. Cylindrical extensions on opposite sides of a gun barrel.

Trysail. Small, triangular, fore-and-aft sail set immediately abaft the foremast, usually during heavy weather.

Tumblehome. Reduction in a ship's beam above the waterline to reduce the weight of her topsides.

Unmoor. A ship moored was held by two anchors; she was **unmoored** by raising one anchor, leaving her riding on the other.

Unship. To remove any object from its normal place.

Upperworks. Hull structure above the level of the topmost gundeck.

Waist. Midpart of the upper deck of the ship.

Wale. Strake, strip or plank standing proud of the rest of the hull.

Warp. Moving a vessel by hauling on ropes.

Way. A ship was under way when she had raised her anchor and was thus exposed to the effects of the wind, tide or current.

Wear, wearing. Altering course by passing the stern through the wind, whilst keeping the sails under full control.

Weather. To sail to windward of an object.

Weather deck. Deck level exposed to the weather.

Weather gage (gauge). To be to the windward of another ship.

Weatherly. The ability of a vessel to sail close to the wind.

Widow's Men. RN ships carried notional "widow's men" ranging from 9 aboard a 1st rate to one for unrated sloops, a financial device to transfer money to a fund to pay pensions to officers' widows.

Windward. That side of the boat from which the wind is coming.

Wolding (also **woolding**). The rope binding around a man-made mast made of sections, which holds the whole together.

Yard. Spar set across a mast, normally used to support a sail.

Yaw. Deviate from the intended course.

LEFT: HMS Victory
(watercolor by an
unknown artist)

INDEX

CREDITS & ACKNOWLEDGEMENTS

The principal photographic source for this work has been the National Martime Museum (NMM), Greenwich, England. The publishers wish to thank David Taylor at the Picture Library of the National Maritime Museum for his help over the time it took to bring everything together. All photographs, paintings and artifacts supplied by the NMM are credited here by page number, position, and reference number.

Front cover: D6099; DD6103; D3920; 8450; D4791; D6033 ; Back cover: BHC1836; **Back flap:** D5219 **1:** PW3758; **2/3:** PW5815; **3:** D6033c; **4:** D6099; **5:** PU6387; **6:** PU4732; **7:** PU0162; **8:** A972; **8/9:** BHC3696; **10:** PW5945; **11 bottom:** PU6119; **14/15:** BHC1836; **16:** PU2366; **17:** A8086; **18:** PW5864; **21:** PU9001; **24/25:** PU5998; **26:** PW5964; **28:** BHSC3203; **30 top:** 196; **30 bottom:** PW5815; **31 top:** PW5030; **31 bottom:** PU8876; **33:** BHC0612; **36:** PU5637; **37:** 6062-42; **38:** PW7970; **39:** B1707; **41:** PX9750; **42:** PU8973; **43:** PU8543; **47:** PW3784; **51:** PU8651; **52:** 3633; **54:** PU6115; **55:** 2417; **56:** PW2387; **57:** PU3519; **58:** C1464; **59:** B3737; **60:** D6099; **61 top:** D6103c; **61 bottom:** D6033c; **65:** D7689_3; **66:** D7689_2; **67 bottom:** D7689_5; **68:** PU4721; **69 bottom:** PW3758; **70 top:** D7689_4; **70 bottom:** PW4969; **71 top:** 437; **72:** PU6037; **73:** PW 7966; **74:** PU5828; **75:** PU6391; **76:** PU6393; **77:** PW8230; **82 top:** PU5516; **83:** BHC1085; **84:** PU6387; **85:** PU7303; **88:** BHC1118; **91:** PU0170; **93:** PY0717